French Huguenots in English-Speaking Lands

Studies in Church History

William L. Fox
General Editor

Vol. 11

PETER LANG
New York • Washington, D.C./Baltimore • Boston • Bern
Frankfurt am Main • Berlin • Brussels • Vienna • Oxford

Horton and Marie-Hélène Davies

French Huguenots in English-Speaking Lands

PETER LANG
New York • Washington, D.C./Baltimore • Boston • Bern
Frankfurt am Main • Berlin • Brussels • Vienna • Oxford

Library of Congress Cataloging-in-Publication Data

Davies, Horton.
French Huguenots in English-speaking lands /
Horton and Marie-Hélène Davies.
p. cm. — (Studies in church history; vol. 11)
Includes bibliographical references (p.   ) and index.
1. Huguenots—Great Britain—History. 2. Huguenots—English-speaking
countries—History. 3. French—English-speaking countries—History.
4. Huguenots—United States—History. 5. French—Great Britain—History.
6. French—United States—History. I. Davies, Marie-Hélène. II. Title.
III. Series: Studies in church history (New York, N.Y.); vol. 11.
DA125.H84D38   941'.0088245—dc21   99-28014
ISBN 0-8204-4542-8
ISSN 1074-6749

Die Deutsche Bibliothek-CIP-Einheitsaufnahme

Davies, Horton:
French Huguenots in English-speaking lands /
Horton and Marie-Hélène Davies.
–New York; Washington, D.C./Baltimore; Boston; Bern;
Frankfurt am Main; Berlin; Brussels; Vienna; Oxford: Lang.
(Studies in church history; Vol. 11)
ISBN 0-8204-4542-8

Cover art: *Noon* by William Hogarth. Graphic Arts Collection, Department of Rare Books and Special Collections, Princeton University Library

Cover design by Lisa Dillon

© 2000 Peter Lang Publishing, Inc., New York

All rights reserved.
Reprint or reproduction, even partially, in all forms such as microfilm,
xerography, microfiche, microcard, and offset strictly prohibited.

Noon by William Hogarth. Credit: Graphic Arts Collection.
Department of Rare Books and Special Collections.
Princeton University Library.

Table of Contents

Introduction ix

1 The Problems of the Huguenots in France 1

2 Persecution: The Necessity to Escape 19

3 Ways of Escape from France 39

4 Huguenot Faith and Character 57

5 Ministers and Doctors; Military Men and Politicians 75

6 The Contributions of Huguenot Manufacturers 95

7 Huguenot Artists and Architects 111

Conclusion 125

Bibliography 129

Index 139

Introduction

The problems confronting the Huguenots when the Edict of Nantes, which had given freedom of thought and expression to their forebears, was revoked, was similar to those of the various victims of the so-called cleansing measures of the twentieth century. For the Huguenots, however, it was spiritual, rather than ethnic, cleansing. They were either to conform to a faith in which they no longer believed or be expelled from the State. Their story is a tribute to the bravery, kindness, intelligence, flexibility, and other qualities that are also imbedded in the human heart.

The geographical scope of the book has been limited to the English-speaking lands, with an occasional reference to South Africa, where English has long been in competition with Afrikaans, so that it cannot be considered an English-speaking land in any exclusive sense. Our limitation to Britain, Ireland and North America is in no sense intended to imply that the Huguenot contributions were unimportant to Switzerland, Prussia, Scandinavia, Russia, Holland, and Belgium where their contributions have merited numerous studies. This study has been restricted because of a need for concentration and because of the wealth and variety of the Huguenot contributions to Britain and its original overseas empire, a large part of which eventually became the United States.

As for time, apart from some enlightening incursions into the past, it is largely limited to the period immediately preceding the Revocation in 1685 until the Edict of Toleration, in 1782. Afterwards, Huguenots had little reason to flee France, since the rising storm of the French Revolution brought another type of reformation that changed the entire political picture.

Chapter 1 outlines the historical background of the problems facing the Huguenots in their own beloved France. Their difficulties began and continued because of both royal and Roman Catholic determination to obliterate tendencies toward Protestantism. The king and the established Church thus condemned the Jansenists, a branch of Catholicism leaning toward the Reformed Church and the Huguenots. The series of attacks on the latter culminated in the Revocation of the Edict of Nantes in 1685. This chapter discusses the struggles of the two religions, as well as the positions of the successive heads of state.

Chapter 2 describes the bitterness of the various forms of persecution the Huguenots suffered. Their maltreatment included increasing exclusions from the professions and vocations in which they had excelled; the requirement that their children be brought up as Roman Catholics from the age of seven; the imprisonment of women who suffered many dreary decades as in the notorious Tour de Constance; the enduring cruelty of the Galleys, where the men of faith served as slaves along with criminals; and the briefer but greater savagery of Hangings and the Wheel.

Chapter 3 concentrates on the often difficult, dramatic, and occasionally ingenious ways the harassed escaped to reach Britain, Ireland and North America.

Chapter 4 analyzes the remarkable fortitude founded on faith in the Huguenot character and its sources in the Bible, its exposition in sermons and the private and family sessions of prayer in Huguenot homes, as well as the features of Calvinist churchmanship.

The remaining chapters analyze the achievements of the Huguenots as ministers of religion, military men, doctors, and politicians (chapter 5), as manufacturers, inventors, and businessmen (chapter 6), and as artists and architects, sculptors and carvers (chapter 7) and how these contributions enriched the English-speaking world.

The conclusion demonstrates that historically, profound belief cannot be exterminated and that Protestantism lived on in France through even the darkest decades, struggling for survival through the sword and the spirit until the Edict of Toleration was promulgated.

Chapter 1

The Problems of the Huguenots in France

National unity, although a laudable goal, has led to some of the most horrible slaughters of history. The story of the progress of Protestantism in Europe, a movement for change and renewal, led to the bloody wars, called the Wars of Religion, which devastated Europe during the sixteenth century. The religious wars were particularly devastating in France and Germany because of the magnitude of the movement. Protestantism eventually changed from a fresh renewal and manageable eccentricity, in the literal sense of the term, to a divisive element that threatened the health of the nation and the equilibrium of national unity. Therefore, instead of collaboration, forces chose sides: authority, hierarchy, reason and stability against individualism, personal experience, intuition, and ferment.[1]

Where did the term *Huguenot* come from? The most credible account of the derivation of the name comes from a pastor, Dr. Collin. He argues that, since the flight of the Waldenses to Geneva in 1535 and of others to England, Strasburg, and Germany, letters from pastor to pastor refering to them secretly as "our Hausgenossen" circulated around Europe. This terminology recalled the Epistle to the Hebrews 21:19, which gave the greeting its force on both sides: "But now we are no more strangers and foreigners, but fellow-citizens with the saints and out of the household of God, built upon the foundation of apostles and prophets, Jesus Christ himself being the chief corner-stone." It became "Gottes Hausegenossen," or "Huisginoz" or "Husknoz" in German or "Huisgenoot" in Dutch.[2]

The Revocation of the Edict de Nantes in 1685 must be viewed in historical perspective. The evangelical movement that started at Meaux encompassed some of the same goals as the Lutheran movement that also spread from Germany across France; simplify the trappings of religion; suppress the statues and images of the saints, reduce the cult of the Virgin to modest proportions, read the prayers in French so that all can understand them, and evangelize the country. The zealous followers of the movement, however, became aggressive and loud. They demanded the destruction of all idols and called the pope anti-Christ. The Church retaliated by cutting their tongues. Thus came the first rebellion of 1524.[3] The wars of religion had begun on a small but increasing scale.

By 1552, La Rochelle had become a stronghold of Protestantism; three men were punished for disturbing the peace by new heresies; two were burned alive, while the third was whipped and expelled. Anne Du Bourg, a noted lawyer, and professor of Law at the University of Orleans and lenient toward the new Protestants, was hanged on 23 December, 1559 on the Place de Grève in Paris. The recording of his death serves as a model and a prelude to the stories concerning the execution of many Huguenots throughout the period after the Revocation of the Edict of Nantes.

> During the journey from the Conciergerie to Place de Grève, the martyr kept all his firmness; but when arrived at the foot of the gallows, while he was taking off his clothes, he could not help uttering deep sighs and crying out "My friends, I am not here as a thief or a murderer; but it is for the sake of the Gospel" He was heard repeating several times: "My God, do not forsake me, for fear that I might forsake you." Immediately after, he was entering with glory into eternity[4]

Perhaps religious dissent might not have assumed such enormous proportions in France had the nobility maintained its initial reluctance to participate. Many noblemen rallied to the Protestant faith after the Treaty of Cateau-Cambrésis, however, as a way to assert their independence from the Catholic king. Thus, political strife branded religious division. Moreover, Protestants did not keep the struggle within the borders of the nation; they also called on Germany, which caused civil division to menace the very fragile national unity striven for in the sixteenth century.

After much mutual slaughter, the struggle took a new turn at the death of Henry III in 1589, leaving only Henry of Navarre, a Protestant, as inheritor to France and unwilling to relinquish his Protestant faith. Seeing his role as mediator and conciliator, Henry agreed to recant and become a Catholic saying that Paris was well worth attending Mass.

In his *Memoirs*, Philippe de Mornay, Sieur de Plessis Marly, a Huguenot nobleman who was adviser to Henry of Navarre, tells of a three-hour conversation with the king partly on the issue of his conversion:

> The long and the short of it all was that he found himself on the very brink of a precipice through the intrigues of some of his own followers, whose names he

mentioned, and saw that his only chance of escape lay in his conversion. But besides this he also said that the Huguenots had not stood by him, as they ought. However he would always regard the reformed faith and those who proposed it just as he had always and he hoped God would have mercy on him."[5]

Through his clever policies, Henry IV regained the favor of the Pope, who forgave him in 1595. He evicted all foreigners from the realm in 1598 and gave back France to the French. Finally, he signed the Edict of Nantes, which granted moderate freedom of worship to the Protestants and restored their rights as French citizens.

The complexity of the Edict of Nantes explains how it contained its own demise. It comprised four documents: ninety-two general articles that were to be perpetual and irrevocable and fifty-six written secret articles, called *particuliers* registered by the Parliament, and two royal *brevets*, which depended on the sole authority of the Crown. The purpose of the Edict, expressed in the Preamble, was to restore the peace between both religions, in order that God

> might be adored and prayed to by all our subjects; if it has not been his will to allow that it should be in one religion, let it be at least under such rules so there will be no trouble nor tumult between them because of it . . .

The Catholics were to have their Mass and their belongings restored where they had been rejected by the Protestants, and the Protestants were to be allowed the enjoyment of public life, liberty of conscience, and public worship in two towns per district, or *baillage*, as well as in the châteaus of Protestant lords; they would be granted four academies for scientific and religious instruction, authority to convoke synods according to the Protestant prescribed method, and a few places of refuge. Protestants would be eligible for all posts and offices as well as receive judicial protection through chambers, half of whose numbers were to be Catholic and the other half Protestant. Poor Protestants would be able to receive alms, be admitted to hospitals, and all could have their children educated. In certain towns, they were able to have their own printers and publishers, which meant that they could propagate their creed.[6]

The Edict was respected during the reign of Henry IV and the Protestants grew stronger, especially through the minority of Louis XIII. They held some of the main positions in the government of the realm. Sully was a competent and trusted minister of Henry IV and of Marie de Medici, until she eventually preferred the corrupt Concini.

Protestants were divided between the cautious, such as Sully and many Parisian worthies, and the tough, who wanted to maintain as many political privileges as they could and were prepared to fight to do so. They tended to be the Protestant clergy, part of the higher nobility, and the majority of the lower nobility, such as Rohan and D'Aubigné. The Prince of Condé became particularly loud, trying to regain the influence and power that he had previously lost. Protestants held strongholds and political assemblies.

During the regency of Marie de Medici, feuds broke out. In 1620, Protestants had rebelled because Catholic worship had been restored in some towns of Béarn. An army under de Luynes was dispatched to conquer Montauban. It failed, and Louis XIII had to compromise with his own people.

Richelieu, Louis XIII's minister, advocated royal absolutism and firmness. Using the pretext that the Protestants were encouraging the English to conquer the island of Ré, he besieged their stronghold, La Rochelle.

A French geographer, Boyer du Parc, made four maps between 1633 and 1642 to indicate the progress of the Protestants in the French realm. They demonstrated that of 270 strongholds of Protestantism, one hundred had a garrison; that Protestant cities remained principally in the south and west of France, or were located on rivers. Boyer du Parc made maps of the four main waterways of France. Protestants controlled a number of bridges over the rivers Loire, Garonne, and Rhône and their confluents, which worried their contemporaries because seas and rivers were the main thoroughfare for commerce.

While Richelieu waged war against the Protestants of France, however he encouraged them outside of France, in England and in Germany, in an attempt to check Spanish power. After the Huguenot defeats of La Rochelle (1627–1628) and Privas (1629), the Edict of Alès, in 1629, revoked the Protestants' political rights while maintaining their civil rights and a limited freedom of worship.[7]

After this defeat, Protestants assumed a very limited role in the urban uprisings that occurred from 1623 to 1631, as well as in the peasant uprisings caused mainly by the levying of further taxation in 1632, 1635, 1636, 1637, and 1645. They seem to have taken no part whatsoever in the civil unrest called the Fronde. This accounts for Louis XIV's favorable view of them as "loyal subjects" at the beginning of the personal reign in 1661.

Thus far, an attempt has been made to place the 1685 Revocation of the Edict de Nantes in its historical context and various phases, before the reign of Louis XIV.

In the early part of the reign of Louis XIV, religious strife consisted mainly of controversy. Preachers argued heatedly with one another from the pulpit. A few overstepped the bounds of courtesy or even of common decency towards their dissident brethren. Some of the contents of the predication earned the repeated remonstrance of the king.[8]

An understanding of the strife between the king, that is temporal power, and the papacy, that is spiritual power, is also basic to understanding the complexity of the Protestant question during the seventeenth century. It often concerned both power and money. The struggles between Louis XIV and the pope over revenues derived from vacant bishoprics, between 1678 and 1693, were certainly relevant to Protestant persecutions. In the north of France, vacant bishoprics brought revenues to the king, whilst in the south they brought in income to the pope. Louis XIV, always in need of money, decided to fight the pope on this issue. A 1682 declaration of four main articles declared that whereas the pope, with the consent of the Church, held spiritual power over the clergy and the faithful of France, the king and the king only ruled temporal matters (that is, finances among others)[9] A battle naturally ensued: Louis XIV named as bishops only priests that would sign this declaration; the pope systematically refused to recognize them. A sacrifice was needed, that would also consolidate the unity of the realm, which was Louis XIV's particular vision. The result was further persecution of the Protestants and of that left-wing part of the Catholic Church, the Jansenists.[10] The king eventually had to back down and let the pope have his way; the Declaration was suppressed in 1693.

Colbert, an economist and Louis XIV's leading minister, was a good friend of the Huguenots. He respected their hard work, dedication, and thrift. He and his son Seignelet did as much as they could to intercede for them. The king however, was pressed by the Church and by another minister, Louvois. In his *Mémoires*, addressed to his son, but with an eye towards posterity, Louis XIV explains his position towards the Protestant question intending to forge spiritual unity among his people. There are allusions to his repression of the mutiny in Vivarais, his sending the Abbé de Bourséis to convert Schomberg and his careful but systematic exclusion policy towards the Huguenots as early as 1661.[11] He resolved, he said,

> not to press them by any new hardship against them, to enforce what they had obtained in previous reigns, but also not to grant them any more and even to circumscribe the execution in the strictest limits that justice and propriety could allow. I named for this, that very year, some officers charged with enforcing the Edict of Nantes . . .

The king continues to explain how he contained Huguenot expansion by suppressing the secret assemblies held in the outskirts of Paris, at Saint Germain, where the fair traditionally took place, at Jamets in the province of Lorraine, and at La Rochelle, where old Protestant families had the right to gather and worship, but where new families had also settled. The king had the new families expelled. He barred Protestants from personal favors, without which one could hardly live under his reign and encouraged the bishops to persuade them to convert. Thus, for instance, Bossuet converted Turenne, the most brilliant general of Louis's armies. In his memoirs, Louis XIV also alludes to other means of persuasion but does not expound on them.[12]

Applying pressure to reduce a people's influence on others has been common practice over the centuries. During the twentieth century, the Germans, the Russians and the Chinese, among others, have used severing the children from their parents and forming them according to the present vision of the State. Many invaders and authoritarian governments have also practiced depriving people of undesirable spiritual leaders.

From the very start of the personal reign, in 1661, a decree in Council fixed the age at fourteen for boys and twelve for girls (that is, the beginning of adolescence and early rebellion) when Protestant children might renounce the Faith of their father. A decree of October 24, 1665, allowed them to ask to live somewhere else than at home and receive quarterly installments for their maintenance. June 17th, 1681, the age became seven years old.

Depriving the Huguenots of educational facilities also came gradually. On November 28, 1664, the new buildings, which the Protestants at Nîmes had added to their college, were handed over to the Jesuits. On April 2, 1666, Protestant noblemen were forbidden to maintain special academies for the education of their children. In November 1667, Protestant schoolmasters were restricted to teaching the children reading, writing and arithmetics. On December 4, 1671, it was decreed that only one school would be maintained in the area where Protestants lived, and each school would have only one master. Measures became more drastic as one approached the fatal date: on June 9, 1681, the academy founded by Coligny at Chatillon-sur-Loing and the academy founded by Henry IV at Sedan were both suppressed. On January 1685, the academy at Saumur was closed followed by the academy at Montauban in March.[13]

The gradual reduction in the number of churches and temples proceeded from the same frame of mind. In Gex in 1662, twenty-three out of twenty-five churches were closed, on the pretext that the territory had been acquired after the Edict of Nantes and that, therefore, the Edict did not apply.

The reduction of attractive callings open to people is also a way of reducing the appeal and propagation of their ideals. Successively, Huguenots were excluded from all civil and municipal charges; as farmers and receivers of taxes, officers of the mint, magistrates, notaries, advocates, marshals, and sergeants. During the early 1660s, the number of notaries at Montpellier was two-thirds Protestant; a decree required that they cease their practice until a proportion of 50/50 was attained. Quotas were also applied to the number of Protestant jewelers. Huguenots were forbidden to advertise as doctors, surgeons, and midwives, or to function as printers, booksellers and clerks. Protestant women could no longer be milliners or laundresses,—the female Hermes of the seventeenth century,— nor could they deliver babies.[14] Their complaints are detailed in the next chapter.

Finally, pressure was also applied to the dying. Priests and magistrates were enjoined to visit any sick Protestant in order to inquire whether they still wanted to die in the Reformed confession or were willing to join the Roman Catholic flock.[15]

The last pressure was applied, in 1681, which became known as "the Dragonnades", introduced by Michel de Marillac, the royal intendant of the generality of Poitiers. He quartered the recusants with a disproportionate number of dragoons who had come back from the wars against Spain and were now idle. They were encouraged to make free with the goods and belongings of Protestant households, although they were officially restrained from committing rape and murder.[16] Descriptions of "the dragonnades" appear in the following chapters.

The vanity of trying to convert souls by force is described eloquently in a colored drawing of 1686: a standing dragoon is threatening a kneeling Huguenot, pen in hand, about to sign his recantation lying on a drum. Left is the caption "Dragon Missionère," under the drum is written "appel évangélique," and on the right, "hérétique signant conversion." To the left of the dragoon is written "qui peut me résister est bien fort," on the musket with a cross in its mouth is written "Raison invincible," on his sword "Raison pénétrante," and on the right is written "La force passe la Raison." On top appears another caption: "nouveaux Missionre (sic) envoyez Par ordre de Louis le Grand par tout le Royaume pour Ramener les Hérétiques à la foy Catholique de la Société de M. de St. Rut, Maréchal de Camp surnommé le Missionnère botté. 1686."[17] Although numbers may not be accurate, it was reported that Marillac obtained thirty-eight thousand conversions through these new missionaries. In Béarn, Foucault writes to Louvois that there remained only one thousand Protestants and that twenty thousand had been converted.[18]

Among Protestant clergy, some could not resist the pressure. Saint Cosme for instance, president of the consistory of Nîmes, abjured secretly before the bishop of Paris; he maintained his function for two years after having abjured and received a pension of a thousand *livres* and the rank of the colonel of the militia.[19] Impressive statistics of conversions were sent to Versailles and from there to the pope, who, before he understood what means were used to effect these conversions, congratulated the king for his Christian zeal. Etienne Patouillet, bishop of Besançon, applauded the activism of the missionaries in his funeral oration for Marie-Thérèse, the Queen:

> She asks God that all the people of her kingdom should be united under one religion and Louis the Great out of the demolished and destroyed Huguenot temples will make monuments to his Piety to give trophies to the Church. That so many souls in Poitou redeemed by the blood of Jesus Christ no longer remain in their blindness so fatal to the state and so deadly for their salvation, and the king with the help of his missionaries, tearing them away from their error, will bring them back to the great light of the truth . . .[20]

The bishop of Grenoble was brave enough to send letters of protestation to the king and impart his concerns to the pope about the means by which conversions were procured. The pope, then, having checked the information, had to send a letter blaming the king of France.

Using physical force was not particularly in keeping with Louis XIV's leadership; he preferred mental and financial starvation. Although, in 1681, he tried to end conversion through violence, eventually, he averted his eyes.[21] His ministers, Colbert and Seignelet on the one hand, and Louvois, on the other, violently disagreed concerning the approach to the Protestant question. Louvois wanted their conversion at all cost, but the king also must have softened his ardor. Letters between Louvois and the officials of Besançon, for instance, show that persecutions by law or dragoons were only a means to obtain conversions. Once obtained, the "New Catholics" were to join again the flock of the loyal subjects of the king.[22]

Numbers he received from intendants only too eager to show that they were efficient may have led the king to believe that there was no longer any Protestant Question in France and that the Edict of Nantes had had its days, as many historians have argued. Still, instead of letting the Edict become obsolete and die a natural death by lack of use, Louis XIV chose to sign an official Revocation. Instead of letting the Protestant faith expire from lack of spiritual fueling, he chose to root it out. Louis XIV's official argumentation appears in the Preamble:

> We have deemed that we could do no better, in order to wipe out totally all memory of troubles, confusion and evils that the progress of this erroneous religion has caused in our realm . . . but to revoke the said Edict of Nantes in its entirety.

In the main, the Edict contained the following injunctions: articles 1, 2 and 3 required the destruction of all temples and public or private assemblies, whether at commoners' or at lords' households. Article 4 required Protestant ministers to leave France within fifteen days, whereas articles 9 and 10 either asked the flown flock to return in order to keep their possessions or forbade the remaining flock to flee, or risk incurring the penalty of the galleys. Article 7 abolished all private Protestant schools and 8 stipulated that children born to Reformed Protestant parents should be baptized by Catholic priests and raised in the Catholic Church.[23] Only Alsace was spared, as the Treaties of Westphalia guaranteed its freedom of worship.

Most people applauded the Revocation. Some saw employment and business opportunities arising from Protestants' flight. Bishops, of course, had to support the king in the name of national and religious unity. But even in some intellectual circles, there was enthusiasm. Madame de Sévigné for instance, in a letter sent to her cousin Bussy-Rabutin, on October 28, 1685 speaks of the Edict in these terms: " Nothing is more beautiful than all it contains, and never has any king done nor will he do anything as memorable."[24]

However, it worried a few far-seeing minds such as Colbert and Seignelet, Vauban, and Saint-Simon, that arch enemy of the policies of Louis XIV, who, in his *Memoirs*, objected much later after the event, in these terms:

> The Revocation of the Edict of Nantes, without the slightest pretext and without any need whatsoever, and the different declarations which ensued were the fruit of this hideous conspiracy, which depopulated a quarter of the kingdom, which ruined its commerce, which weakened it in all its parts, which submitted it for so long to the public and avowed ransacking of dragoons, which authorized the torments and tortures by which they really caused the death of innocent people of both sexes by the thousands . . . which handed out our manufactures to foreigners.

Saint-Simon continues by giving a vivid description of Huguenot fugitives. He depicts them naked, wandering in search of food, drink, and shelter, the strong and the frail, the commoner, and the nobleman . . ."[25] The king had to forbid dumping the corpses of dead Huguenots for fear of sedition, but the practice continued.

Voltaire in *Le Siècle de Louis XIV* (Vol. 29) alludes to it briefly: "If he had not believed that his will was enough to make one million men change religions, France would not have lost so many citizens." Louis XIV was intelligent enough to listen to the arguments of Seignelet and Vauban, whilst following the policy of Louvois. He tried to limit emigration. There were antiemigration laws for every one between 1669 and 1680 but the decrees of May 18 and July 14, 1682, concerned Protestants in particular; they were threatened by confiscation of property and imprisonment. Another decree around this time, which was renewed every three years until 1778, forbade them to sell their property for three years, once they had left the realm. From 1685, the attempt, if they were caught, was punished by incarceration, confinement in the galleys, or deportation to the West Indies.[26] As Protestants then sought to master the navy, in June 1686, it was decreed that foreign ships helping them flee would be confiscated, and an edict of November 20, 1687, forbade a ship to leave France, if two-thirds of the crew were not Catholics. On land in Béarn in 1686, there was a reward of twenty *écus* for each Protestant caught. By 1687, however, officers on the borders wearied of having to punish the innocent, prisons were full, and surveillance was relaxed. Severity and leniency alternate in this way, until the final edict of Toleration in 1787.[27]

The authorities of the provinces of France varied in their enthusiasm about following the royal decrees. The parliament of Franche-Comté seems to have been particularly zealous; that of Montpellier was only sporadically obedient for instance. The intendant of Normandy, M. De Gourgnes, believed that educating the children would prevent the parents from emigrating.[28] Louis XIV also had to make exceptions: Admiral Du Quesne was allowed to die peacefully in France, although his sons escaped to Switzerland. General Schomberg was invited to stay, but left, shaking the mud off his boots. The more powerful and loud the Protestant heretic was, the better chance he or she had of being allowed to flee. On February 1, 1686, for the sake of commerce, the king had to make an exception and allow foreign traders of the Protestant confession to enter France without going through the bureaucratic harrassment of having to declare when they entered and when they left.

Parliaments in France were kept busy. The year of his death, in 1715, Louis XIV proudly announced that he had cut off all the heads of the dissenting hydra, and put an end to all Protestant worship in France. Yet, less than half a year later, while the king lay dying in Versailles, at the gate of the city of Nîmes, a worship service and protest meeting called the FIRST SYNOD OF THE DESERT was held by dissident Huguenots, who began to reorganize the Protestant Church.[29]

The reaction of foreign courts also varied. All Protestant states, some of which were former allies of France, manifested their displeasure. The Dutch and the Swedes linked up with the Elector of Brandenburg into the Ligue of Augsburg where France would eventually have to fight its own former army in the hostilities that began in 1688. There was the usual official denial of wrongdoing from James II, king of England and a friend of Louis XIV, though he let congregations pick up collections for Huguenot relief. At his court, François Usson de Bonrepaux, gave gratuities on behalf of Louis XIV to win them back: he persuaded 507 of them, including 27 naval officers, 354 sailors, and 106 craftsmen. Under William III and Queen Anne, England took stronger steps; it blamed France for its intolerance and showed great kindness to its refugees.

Official informers existed, Fonant and Roberts in London, for instance, and Tillières in Holland. Tillières worked from Harlem, and covered the whole of Holland. A former Protestant, he was trusted by all including the famous pastor Claude and his son. From September 1685, for three years, until his death, he was the indefatigable informer to the king's ambassador, le Comte d'Avaux, who, in turn, spied on his spy.

Thanks to the interception of letters and the coded messages he received, Tillières was able to denounce by name those who led and organized Protestants to freedom as well as to give the dates and locations of their arrivals and departures. This was passed on to Colbert by the ambassador d'Avaux and enabled the king to realize how many "religionnaires" were trying to leave the realm, to proceed to a number of arrests, and to discourage the faint-hearted. Tillières became a rich man, paid handsomely by d'Avaux and by the spoils he appropriated from monies entrusted to him. His life was brief, however: when he tried to persuade refugees to return to France, once they had experienced the hardships of settling without funds, he became suspicious to them.[30]

The following chapters will detail the sufferings and flight of the Huguenots in and out of the French realm. Some of them settled, with various degrees of success, in societies whose customs were foreign to them. Many who could not, or would not, travel recanted: those who were lukewarm and those whose hands and lips recanted, but whose hearts did not change. The abjuration not only asked them to betray their faith, it also made informing on their friends a civic duty. Many underwent terrible guilt feelings similar to those of the relatives of deceased soldiers or prisoners of war, sometimes triggered by the poignant letters they received from family abroad. Some disappeared untraced; of others, one had news only second or third hand. Such was Pierre Durand deported on *La Concorde* to the Antilles, who ended up in a hospital in Martinique. His wife and children sought refuge in Switzerland.[31]

The Protestants who were still alive in France eventually formed a resistance movement in the Cévennes. They were led by pastor Vivens. who had fled to Holland and the mystic Brousson, who had trained in Lausanne and was the last of the core of the French pastors to return to France under the most perilous circumstances.[32]

Later Jean Cavalier and Antoine Court led the movement. The latter started a seminary around 1730 in Lausanne called The School for the Ministers of the Désert. Protestants held assemblies on the plateau and in the woods, mainly under the direction of laymen, as most of the pastors had fled.[33] Assemblies were frequently disrupted, as at La Salle where 300 died in 1689, and the faithful were cruelly tortured by intendant Basville, encouraged by the Abbé du Ceyla. Prophetism was strong and the stern sense of discipline had disappeared.

Eventually, the movement changed from pacifism to militarism, and the peasants of the Cévennes revolted (1702–1705). They were ridden with the guilt of apostasy and the need to act against the oppressor who was also burdening them with too many taxes. They were called Camisards, because they wore white shirts over their clothes for recognition.

On July 24, 1702, Cévenol peasants murdered the Abbé du Ceyla or Cheila. The insurrection first led by Séguier and Laporte destroyed Catholic churches and slaughtered some of the priests. Seventy per cent of the taxes were paid late. Madame la Baronne de Charnisay describes the organization of the guerilla army of the Camisards, which forced the trained army of the king to capitulate. Four chiefs commanded each troop and made incursions in different areas. They were young men who had only learned about the dragonnades by hearsay. Cavalier had the highest reputation: he commanded a thousand men and covered the area between Alès and Andouze, and demonstrated his talent for strategy during the battle of Martignargues in 1703. Higher up in the area, Roland commanded the second most famous troop, with 200 men; from La Salle to Saint André-de-Valborgne. Above, de la Roze succeeded in command to Castanet. At the foot of Mont Lozère, Nicholas, alias Joanin des Plaus, was in charge.[34]

The Reformers eventually found themselves in the situation of being Christians without a Church. From 1707, one knew that Protestantism would not completely die in France; the Refugees published *Le Théâtre Sacré des Cévennes*. In 1715, Antoine Court, wishing to reestablish the Discipline and the use of the Consistory, the Elders, and the Synods, decided to consider as a synodal assembly a secret reunion of seven to eight preachers held in a village of the Lower Cévennes. Others followed, and the provincial synods were reconstituted. In 1726, the first national synod of the Désert was held in Vivarais, and the Protestant Church was replanted.[35] In 1724, a royal declaration recognized the need to codify repressive measures in reference to those who attended assemblies and their pastors. By 1735, the work of the pastors of the Désert reached Haut-Languedoc and the district of Montauban. In 1744, an important national Synod at Ledignan in Bas Languedoc included representatives from seven provinces, including those of Poitou and Normandy.

The presence of Antoine Court avoided a schism fomented by Pastor Boyer from the Cévennes. The years 1745–1746 saw a recrudescence of persecution; three pastors were executed, a number of the faithful were sent to the galleys, and the women were incarcerated in the Tour de Constance. Antoine Court died in Lausanne in 1760.[36]

The history of the persecutions continued, but, in the 1760s, popular opinion no longer tolerated such violence. Three affairs at that time gained national publicity: that of Pastor Rochette, who was apprehended for the wrong reason, but showed his registry of Protestant marriages and baptism to prove his innocence by which, ironically, he gave proof of being an illegal Protestant minister. He and his supporters, the three Grenier brothers, were hung publicly in 1762. The same year saw the Calas affair, a father falsely accused of having killed his son to prevent his turning Catholic. He was tortured, killed, and his body dragged through the streets that very same year. Then came the case of Sirven in 1764, also accused of having murdered a child to stop her recanting. Luckier than the other two, he managed to flee into Switzerland and was rehabilitated, as was Calas's reputation, thanks to Voltaire. In the 1770s, the last Protestants incarcerated for the sake of religion were released. At court, Louis XVI employed a Geneva Protestant, Necker, who became an unofficial minister of finances. Popular opinion was ripe for the advent of the Edict of Toleration.

The Edict of Toleration was the result of gradual decline of Christian belief in eighteenth century France and the progress of sensualism and materialism. The country was influenced by the philosophy of Locke which emphasized experience and observation. The progress of science and the return to nature led to belief in a God who was a clockmaker, not the immanent savior of each and every soul as Christianity maintains. Hence, the partisans of "Grace is contrary to Nature" would wane, and Deism arose. The sensualists would find the God of poverty, chastity, and obedience most inconvenient. Jansenism had been suppressed, the Protestants were still occasionally persecuted. Priests became often attracted by Mammon, which caused the downfall of those who had adapted the Gospel to the needs of the powerful in order to save the influence of the Church: the Jesuits. There was Father Valette, the great tycoon of the Antilles, or Cardinal de Rohan who was the butt of satire of the Press. As in such times of faith crisis, superstition was on the rise, and magic ceremonies were performed. Oriental cults appeared in Paris. The Edict of Toleration (1787) sought to accommodate all beliefs.[37]

The Edict of Toleration was not a resurgence of the Edict of Nantes. It did not provide the Protestants with official places for worship. It merely made them citizens, able to register births, marriages, and deaths in front of a civilian magistrate. It showed that priests were no longer the official keepers of State records. Demographically, Protestants were no longer a threat. They formed only one-fiftieth of the population of France.[38]

Notes

1. George A. Rothrock. *The Huguenots: A Biography of a Minority,* (Chicago: Nelson Hall, 1979), 56 f.

2. Dr. Collin, "Concerning the Name Huguenot," *P.H.S.L.* 6, 1898-1901, 327-355.

3. Pierre Miquel, *Histoire de la France,* (Paris: Fayard, 1977), 160ff.

4. Eugène et Emile Haag. *La France protestante.* 5 vols. (Paris: Fischbacher, 1877-86), vol. 5, col. 594.

5. Arbaleste de Mornay, *A Huguenot Family in the XVIth century: The Memoirs of Philippe de Mornay,* (London: Routledge, 1926), 273-74.

6. N. M. Sutherland, *The Huguenot struggle for recognition,* (New Haven & London: Yale University Press, 1980), 328-30. The book also contains an excellent analysis of the political tensions, which led to the Edict. See also Rothrock, *The Huguenots,* 125 f.and Louis Delmas, *The Huguenots of La Rochelle,* transl. by George L Catlin, (New York: Anson D.F. Randolph and Co., 1880), 111-12.

7. Emile, G. Léonard, *Histoire du Protestantisme* (Paris: P.U.F., 1955), 84-86. An interesting compilation of the maps of Boyer du Parc appears in Jean Michaud, *Histoire. 1492-1789. La Renaissance et les Temps Modernes,* (Paris: Hachette, 1970), 169.

8. See for instance about Pierre du Moulin in *B.S.H.P.F.,* vol. 40, 222 and 109, and 164-67.

9. Léon Mention, *Documents relatifs aux rapports du clergé avec la royauté* (Reprint Geneva: Stakine-Megeriotis, 1976.) See also Louis XIV, *Mémoires,* ed. by Jean Longnon. (Paris: Tallandier, 1978), 202-05.

10. To learn the opinions of the papacy on the issue see André Latreille. "La Révocation de l'Edit de Nantes vue par les nonces d'Innocent XI," in *B.S.H.P.F.,* vol. 103, 229ff.

11. Louis XIV, *Mémoires,* (Paris: Tellandier, 1978), 202ff.

12. Louis XIV, *Mémoires,* 77-78.

13. Charles Baird, *History of the Huguenot emigration to America* (New York: Dodd, Mead and Co., 1885), 247-249. See also Henry Baird, *Huguenots of the Revocation of the Edict of Nantes,* (New York: Scribners, 1895), vol. 1, 81. A balanced point of view will also recall that, as professions were often acquired by network, in Protestant strongholds, there was reverse discrimination, and Catholics tended to be excluded.

14. C. Baird, *Ibid.*

15. Montesquieu alludes ironically to Louis XIV's mass propaganda claiming that the Huguenots were taking all the good positions that Catholics should have in *Lettres Persanes* (1721), letter LXXXV, where the Persians persecute the Armenians in order to suppress all the best merchants of the realm . . .

16. Henry Baird, *Huguenots of the Revocation*, vol. 1, 505 f.

17. Bibliothèque Nationale. Cabinet des Estampes.

18. Camille F.M.Rousset, *Histoire de Louvois et de son administration politique et militaire*, (Paris: Didier, 1862–64), vol. 3.

19. C. A. De Janzé. *Les Huguenots* (Paris: Grassart, 1886), 18.

20. Etienne Patouillet, *Oraison funèbre de Marie-Thérèse d'Autriche* (Besançon: Rigoine, 1683).

21. Bertran van Ruymbekia, "The Huguenots and the early colonization of South Carolina" in *Proceedings of the Huguenot Society of South Carolina*, vol. 95. The author is excellent in giving the list of the edicts incrimentally eliminating all Huguenot power.

22. Jean-Marc Debard, "Révocation de l'Edit de Nantes et abjurations: les prisonniers huguenots de Besançon (1686–1688)." *B.S.H.P.F.*, vol. 131, 508–520.

23. Henry M. Baird. *The Huguenots and the Revocation of the Edict of Nantes*, Vol. 2. and François A. Isembert, *Recueil général des anciennes lois françaises* (Paris: Belin-le Prieur, 1821–1833), vol. 19 of 29 Vols.

24. See also Nicole Ferrier-Caverivière. "La littérature encomiastique et la Révocation de l'Edit de Nantes" in *B.S.H.P.F.* Vol. 131.

25. De Janzé. *Les Huguenots: Cent ans de persecution, 1685–1789*, (Paris: Grassart: 1886), 37–38. Saint-Simon's comments take into consideration the already known results of the Edict of Nantes, as he was only ten when the event occurred. Later, apart from those, such as Montesquieu and Voltaire who voiced their opinion directly on the Huguenot question, there were many literary allusions to the persecution of the Huguenots, in Marivaux *Le Télémaque travesti*, for instance, and in a number of works of Prévost, such as in *Le Pour et le Contre*, IX, 226–27, *Les Mémoires et aventures d'un homme de qualité*, 135, Cleveland pursues his studies at the Academy of Saumur; in the *Doyen de Killerine*, he parallels French and English intolerance by alluding to the English repression of the Irish Catholics.

26. Elie Benoit. *Histoire de l'Edit de Nantes*, (London: Dunton, 1694), vol. 5, 976.

27. Bertran van Ruymbekia, "The Huguenots and the early colonization of South Carolina". *Proceedings of the Huguenot Society of South Carolina*, vol. 95.

28. "Les privilèges des Protestants en Basse-Normandie" *B.S.H.P.F.*, vol. 45, 76ff.

29. Rothrock, *The Huguenots*, 177 f.

30. See Warren C. Scoville, *The persecution of the Huguenots and French economic development, 1680–1720* (Berkeley: University of California, 1960), 155 f. On Tillières, see Jacques Sole. "La diplomatie de Louis XIV et les protestants français réfugiés aux Provinces Unies, 1679-1688." *B.S.H.P.F.*, vol. 115, 641-43.

31. "Pierre Durand Régent d'Ecole aux Cévennes (1630-1690) Pierre Faisses et autres régents cévenols." *B.S.H.P.F.*, vol. 111, 23-45 f.

32. Henry M Baird, *The Huguenots and the Revocation*, vol 2, 210. On Claude Brousson's life see Ligou, *Le Protestantisme en France* (Paris: Société d'Edition d'Enseignement Supérieur, 1968), 260 ff. He helped to organize the refugees in many parts of Europe, returned to France in 1689, stayed two years in Languedoc, returned to Holland, went to England, and, in 1695, returned to France, had to flee to Switzerland in 1696, and returned to Vivarais until 1698. See also, *B.S.H.P.F.*, vol. 34.

33. On the Church of the Désert, see Eugène & Emile Haag, *La France Protestante*, vol 2, columns 926-941, and vol. 4, cols. 809-22; Ligou, *Le Protestantisme en France*, 250-267, ending on the main episodes of the war of the Camisards; Browning, *A History of the Huguenots* (Philadelphia: Lee and Blanchard, 1845) 390-412.

34. *Un Gentilhomme Huguenot au Temps des Camisards. Le Baron d'Aigaliers par Madame la Baronne de Charnisay.* (Mas Soubeyran: Musée du Désert, 1935), 130-34. On the Camisards, see also Ligou, *Le Protestantisme en France de 1598 à 1715*, 260-268.

35. *Les Huguenots. Exposition nationale.* (Paris: Archives nationales: 1985-1986.)

36. Henry Baird, *Huguenots and the Revocation*, 18-20.

37. See also Henry M Baird, "The Recovery of religious liberty by the Huguenots." *Proceedings of the Huguenot Society of America*, vol. 3, 37-51.

38. Jean Michaud, *Histoire de France. 1482-1789. La Renaissance et les temps modernes* (Paris: Hachette, 1974), 344.

Chapter 2

Persecution: The Necessity to Escape

People emigrate for different reasons—new opportunities, marriages to foreigners, or work assignments abroad. This chapter examines the reasons that so many Huguenots emigrated, but it concentrates on the primary reason—persecutions. This cruelty extended gradually to ever larger groups of people. Persecution is investigated, as it appears in two major categories—violence directed toward entire families of Protestants and violence experienced by individual Huguenots. Both forms of persecution—individual and familial—will be illustrated in detail.

The forms of persecutions towards Protestant families though listed in the previous chapter must be detailed in this chapter. The repression of the Huguenots occurred in successive stages. How it worsened is evidenced by the fact that Louis XIV directed twelve Acts against what was then called the "Pretended Reformed Church" from 1661 to 1679, whereas an additional eighty-five were issued from 1679 to 1685.

First their public worship was proscribed; a hundred of their temples were destroyed, starting in Poitou, Provence, and the county of Gex in 1659, and only two remained in Brittany. The letters of John Locke give an interesting historical perspective on the restrictions applied to the Reformed, which confirm from a personal point of view the trends seen in chapter 1. During a visit to Nîmes on January 3, 1676, he notes that the Protestants of Nîmes are left with only one temple; that out of the four consuls, two are Catholics; that the two Protestant consuls can no longer wear their robes at Holy Communion; that the Protestants have been despoiled of their hospital, and that they no longer use the hospital room that was left them because Catholic priests would harass the patients. On January 18, while visiting Montpellier, he notes that the Protestants of Uzès are no longer allowed to send a deputy to the Assembly of Montpellier, and that their only remaining temple is going to be destroyed, because it was built too near the Catholic Church which caused the singing of psalms to disturb the Mass. On February 1, he notes that, although the Protestants pay the same taxes as the Catholics, they can no longer exercise public offices, and that, during the last ten years, at least sixty temples have been demolished, but on February 13, 1679, having reached Paris, he raises the number to 300 for the last twenty years. On February 21, he notes that the king has just forbidden mixed marriages and that, at church, many people coughed in protest.[1]

Harassments included prohibiting the public and even the private singing of the Psalms, creating houses for the propagation of the Catholic faith in Protestant cities like Wassy, having missionaries, during Protestant services, read a letter from the king ordering the ministers of RPR to grant their congregations the freedom to go to Mass. . . .[2]

Finally, there was the Revocation of the Edict in 1685, when all temples were destroyed and their pastors banished from the realm. All born henceforth were to be registered, baptized, and reared in the Catholic religion, otherwise the parents would be fined five hundred *livres*. Some parents had already foreseen disaster and sent their children to England or Holland to friends or relatives.[3]

Louis XIV tried to crush the seeds of Protestantism by regulating the education of children. In 1665, parents were forced to pay for the Catholic education of a child whom the advantages offered by conversion "had seduced from his father's religion."[4] In 1666, Protestant nobles were forbidden to maintain academies for the instruction of their children. Children at the age of seven were sent away to be brought up as Catholics. In 1670, Protestant schoolmasters were restricted to teaching children, reading, writing, and arithmetic. In 1681, the Academy founded by Coligny at Chatillon sur Loing and the Academy of Sedan founded by Henry IV were both suppressed. In 1685 the Academies of Saumur and Montauban were also closed.[5]

Financial pressures occurred gradually. A number of Huguenots under the previous reigns and the early reign of Louis XIV had held important positions—thus, Sully became prime minister, Schomberg and Ruvigny were marshals of France and Abraham Du Quesne Lord Admiral, to list only a few. Like Turenne, they had to embrace the Catholic faith. There were promises of reward to those who would recant from the *Caisse des Conversions*, engineered by Pélisson-Fontanier as a good way to please the papacy (November 1, 1676).[6] The program failed for various reasons, one of which was that money was sometimes given without instruction.

Another pressure was the ejection of Huguenots from all the lucrative professions or occupations for which they had qualified, such as medicine and law. In La Rochelle, doctors complained of having been barred from the medical corps. For instance, Jean Seignette, Elie Richard and Elie Bouhéreau, having been excluded from the College of Medicine could no longer practice their art. Bouhéreau was a particularly distinguished example. Educated at Saumur, doctor in medicine from the University of Orange, a translator of Origen, offered a chair of philosophy at Saumur in 1684, he was banished to Poitiers and was allowed by favor to reside in Paris in August 1685. He appealed in July 1683 in the name of all three, but was firmly answered that "no physician will be included in the Body and College of La Rochelle, unless they are Catholics."[7]

In the eighteenth century, one of the most renowned examples of Protestants converting in order to be able to practice the legal profession was the case of two sons of Calas—one had converted for that very same reason, whereas the other was thinking of getting a certificate of attendance from a vicar in order to be allowed to continue his studies.

Several other professions and occupations for which heads of household were trained and in which they had proved their competence were now unavailable to them. Successively they were excluded from all civil and municipal charges, as farmers and receivers of taxes, officers of the Mint, magistrates, notaries, advocates, marshals, and sergeants. Nor were they permitted to function as printers, booksellers, clerks, and public messengers. Huguenot women were forbidden to act as nurses, midwives, or milliners. Catholic members were commanded to repel the Huguenots from these appointments. The Revocation of the Edict of Nantes added further that all aristocrats supporting Protestantism would lose their estates.

As the spiritual and economic starvation pressures did not effect enough conversions, an officer of the army of Louvois suggested as the final and most brutal attempts to persuade whole families to become Catholic: the dragonnades.[8] By law, villages were to host the soldiers of armies coming back from war. Louvois agreed that it would be expedient to select Protestant families for the hosting and to exempt Catholic families. Their conduct as "booted missionaries" would be unrestrained by their officers who would encourage them to bleed the Protestant resources until they might convert. Thus, they wrecked their homes and their contents and tortured the man, and sometimes raped his wife and his children from 1681 to 1689, as we shall see in detail.

It is interesting to consider the parts played by the clergy in these persecutions. Friendships often existed between the spiritual shepherds of both religions: the difficulty of educating the flock spiritually was a common bond. Such friendships sometimes survived the distance created by severe laws and the distance of emigration. Such appears in a letter in verse and in patois, for instance, from Pierre Fargues, alias Tristan, a refugee in London to a friend of his, a priest at Mas-d'Azil, in Ariège, which both reassures his friend on the happy settlement of the minister and his family and propagandizes the virtues of the Reformed religion.[9] The sadism of others, such as the Abbé de Cheyla, whose death marked the beginning of the war of the Camisards, has already been mentioned.

Two bishops of adjacent dioceses were antithetic to each other and show that the persecution of the Protestants had further consequences—that of dividing the Catholic clergy of France. Daniel de Cosnac, Bishop of Valence, had as a main concern to root out the heresy of Protestantism, by destroying eighty temples in 1683 and the remaining ones in 1685. He believed that the unique source of the clergy's unhappiness was heresy, which derived from Luther and Calvin, weakened the Church's jurisdiction and usurped the clergy's revenues. He, therefore, was completely in favor of the "booted missionaries."[10] The other was the Bishop of Grenoble, Etienne Le Camus. A priest at the court, he was also eager to end Protestant heresy. Yet, he refused to employ violence, nor did he accept forced conversions, which, in his eyes, were worthless.[11]

Many letters, tracts, and narrations exemplify the brutality that affected the largest group of Huguenots, the descent of the "booted missionaries", the dragoons, on their homes. They relate the arrival of these soldiers, with their swords in their hands, crying, "Kill! Kill! Or else be Catholics!" Jean Claude, formerly minister at Charenton, paints a vivid and pathetic picture of their arrival and its consequences in an extensive catalogue of their cruelties. He writes:

> The troops immediately seized on the gates and avenues of the cities; they placed guards in all the passages, and often came with their swords in their hands. They were quartered among the Reformists at discretion with a strict charge, that none should depart out of their houses, nor conceal any of their goods or effects, on great penalties, even on the Catholicks, that should receive or assist them in any manner. The first days were spent in consuming all provisions the house afforded and taking from them whatever they could see, money, rings, jewels and in general, whatsoever was of value. After this they pillaged the family, and invited not only the Catholicks of the place, but also those of neighboring cities and towns, to come and buy the goods and other things that would yield money. Afterwards they fell on their persons, and there's no wickedness or horror which they did not put in practice to force them to change their religion.
>
> Amidst a thousand hideous cries, and a thousand blasphemies, they hung men and women by the hair or feet on the roofs of the chamber, or chimney-hooks, and smookt them with whisps of wet hay, till they were no longer able to

bear it and when they had taken them down, if they would not sign, they hung them up immediately again. They threw them on great fires kindled for the purpose; and pulled them not out till they were half roasted. They tyed ropes under their arms and plunged them to and again into wells, from which they would not take them till they had promised to change their religion. They tyed them as they do criminals, put to the question; and in this posture, with a funnel filled with wine, poured it down their throats, till the fumes of it depriving them of their reason, they made them say they would consent to be Catholicks. They stript them naked, and after having offered them a 1000 infamous indignities, they stuck them with pins from the top to the bottom. They cut them with penknives, and sometimes with red hot pincers, took them by the nose, and dragged them about their rooms, till they promised to become Catholicks, or that the cries of these poor wretches, that in this condition call'd on God for their assistance, constrained them to let them go.

They beat them with staves and dragged them all bruis'd to the churches where their bare forced presence was accounted for an abjuration. They held them from sleeping seven or eight days, relieving one another to watch them night and day and keep them waking. They threw buckets of water on their faces and tormented them 1000 ways, holding over their heads kettles turned downwards, whereon they made a continual noise, till these poor creatures had even lost their senses . . .

It happened in some places, that they tyed fathers and husbands to the bedposts, and before their eyes forced their wives and daughters. In another place, rapes were publickly and generally permitted for many hours together. They plucked off the nails from the hands and toes of others, which could not be endured without intolerable pain. They burnt the feet of others. They blew up men and women with bellows even till they were ready to burst.[12]

As they were performing these cruelties, the military "guests" supplied themselves with cash by selling domestic animals, furniture, and movable property. The consequence was, as Henry Dupont asserts "to stimulate emigration to an unparallelled extent . . ."[13] Theoretically, all was permitted to the soldiers, except rape and killing, but De Janzé claims that this instruction was a dead letter, as attested both by Elie Benoit and Jurieu.[14]

From these general accounts of the dragonnades we proceed to individual experiences. In Normandy, the 200 dragoons lodged in the home of the baron of Neufville three times a week put the furniture of his castle up for sale and promised his Lady that if she did not abjure, they would sell the forest and the land. At the castle of Ramsay, in Brittany, it was discovered when the soldiers had made their exit, that they had left behind only two small worn cabinets, an old cupboard and some bundles of firewood. Peshels of Montauban reported that when the soldiers had taken from his home the andirons, a shovel, tongs and iron pokers—the last debris of his home— they went to pillage his farms from which they stole the animals to sell them. Pechels wrote: "They often threatened to demolish my house to sell it for its materials. Finally there was fixed on my door a paper signed by the Intendant notifying that the soldiers would be lodged at my cost in an inn."[15]

One housewife, who later escaped to England, wrote the following account of dragooning, stressing the sheer waste. The dragoons were . . .

> gorging themselves, drinking the wine and throwing away the rest, giving food to cats and dogs, giving the bread and the wheat to the pigs and horses, burning what is combustible, lowering and destroying the roofs, demolishing and burning the houses, beating and clubbing the people . . . choking them with smoke, making them freeze with water from a well, tearing their hair from their heads and from the beard with pincers, pulling out their nails with tongs, stabbing their bodies with pins, hanging them by their hair, by their armpits, by their feet and by the neck, attaching them to the foot of a tree and killing them there, roasting them on a fire like meat on a spit, throwing flaming grease on their naked body . . .[16]

Jeanne Terrasson provides a full account of the dragonnades in her memoirs. A Sunday in September 1685, saw the arrival in Dié, Dauphiné, of soldiers, in her place of birth, sent by the Catholics to constrain those of her faith to renounce it. In this situation, many Protestants fled into fields, woods, and even caves, among whom was her husband. Outside her home, she met two women, both of her family, ready to abdicate to save their homes, informing her that the soldiers were only three hours away. She was committed to her faith in Divine protection. Eventually, ten soldiers lodged in her house, with only her husband's uncle to keep her company. She was approached by a regimental officer, who told her, in a moderate fashion, that it was necessary to obey the king and accept the good religion, adding that if she did not obey, he would have to sell their goods to the soldiers until they would have eaten everything, but if she accepted the conditions, it would cost her nothing. At the same time, he asked if she was single. She replied in the negative, and then a soldier said, "She had told us she has a husband who without doubt is hiding elsewhere." After a long contest, the officer, seeing he could gain nothing from her, put in writing a list of all that he found valuable in the house and commanded the soldiers to guard them with care. Finally, he said to her: "You are unwilling to obey the orders of the king with gentleness; you'll have to do it by force." To which she replied in all gentleness:

> Sir, as long as the King requires nothing that goes against my conscience, nor against the obedience I owe to God, I am ready to obey him. But as soon as the

orders of the king oblige me to violate the Divine Law, then I shall follow the maxim of the apostle and I shall say without fear that it is better to obey God than men."

After a night of anxiety, the next morning, she went to hide among friends. Returning home, she saw forty soldiers about the house, who turned its lower level into a stable and put their horses there, and made the rest of the house a kind of retreat. They sold all the furniture except what was in the basement. After expressing all their rage, they left the house, not allowing anyone to shut the doors. Finally, her husband, who admired her courage and faith and was ashamed of his own weakness, rejoined her.

A parallel experience of the dragoons, but with a different ending, was that of Pierre Lambert Beauregard, who was sixty-eight years old. In 1685, he was told to keep the dragoons in his house until he recanted. He got thirty-six soldiers who swore a great deal. After sixteen days he had to sell his furniture in order to feed them, which was costing him fifty-three *livres* a day, including the hay for their horses. They dragged his wife around the town until she recanted. They threatened to cut the nose and ears of her daughters and they were sent to convents. They gave Pierre time to think things over, but, as he remained obdurate, they returned because he still owned a fine house and forty sheep. Next he received the rough treatment. They burnt his feet by applying the red shovel to his soles and putting his shoes on. He forgives them, but he is then sent to prison. He abjures to give himself time to think, but there's a decree to keep him in prison. The archbishop, however, comes to console him and allows his son to return to help him.[17]

Finally, we shall consider the experience of Sieur Thomas Bureau of Niort in a letter written to his brother in London, a bookseller. He saw the nastiness of the dragoons in a nearby town, fearing the same would happen at Niort. His brother-in-law, who accompanied him, resolved to go to Niort, but he said:

> But the dragoons were there already, committing the most extraordinary outrages. This prevented my entering the town; my brother-in-law did so, because being the head of a household, it would have been criminal to have absented himself; as soon as the dragoons were in the town, four of them were sent to our house: they began with the shop, throwing all the books on the ground, then with hammers and axes, broke into pieces all the framework of the shop, the shelves, the glass and the woodwork, brought their horses in and let them use the books as their litter. They went next into the bedrooms and threw everything into the street . . . The mayor watched this from his front door, delighting in it all.

He leaves, in order to try to get help from Paris, but his mother reports that she can endure it no longer. She informs him that she can no longer meet the costs of the excessive spending of the dragoons, for, apart from the four crowns she gives them each day, they have consumed all her silver plate. The narrative continues thus:

> The commandant of the dragoons, coming to our house last night, called my mother and said to her "What! You bitch! You have not yet changed your religion, nor your whore of a daughter!" to which my mother answered that she hoped by the grace of God never to deny Him. "Well then", he said, "damned bitch, you shall soon be hanged along with eight or ten stubborn persons in this town who are no more willing to change than you." The dragoon said it would be better to fasten their horses' halters around their necks and drag them through the streets like mad dogs to serve as an example . . . The mayor told my mother that if she left her house, even for six hours, he would have her hanged and that they were going to take all the books that were in our shop to the Square in front of the Chateau and burn them "I am exhorting my mother not to be daunted by all this and to continue as she has so well begun." He adds that "Monsieur Perrault senior and Messrs. Nérichau are emprisoned in dungeons, with irons on their feet for merely having said that they were good and faithful servants of the King, but that they would never change their Religion."[18]

All good and faithful servants of the king did not meet with the same fate, although all became reprobates. Du Quesne, admiral of the French fleet, was allowed to remain in France, while retaining his Protestant faith, but his two sons found it safer to go to Switzerland. Others were tried and hanged, or burned at the stake. Although the fate of all Protestants was sealed by the Revocation of the Edict in 1685, the penalties varied from individual to individual.

After the Revocation, some men were incarcerated; others underwent expeditious trials, were tortured, executed and finally dragged in the street, for their bodies to be discarded on the public dump[19] Those who were incarcerated were often transferred from the location where they were caught in order to avoid civil unrest. Thus, for instance, prisoners caught from the island of Ré were transferred to a prison in Lourdes near the Spanish border.[20]

As the years passed, Louis XIV devised a more economical way to punish Protestants who would not recant. We know from a letter written by Louvois to his subordinate Baville that the king now considered it more convenient to dispense with the declaration by which he had condemned to death all attending Protestant assemblies.[21] Instead, the men were to be sent to serve in the galleys, and the women were forced to spend mind-boggling years incarcerated either in convents, where they knew the hard treatment "for the good of their souls" or in the famous Tour de Constance. If, in the galleys, they refused to bow as the Host of the Mass passed by or was elevated, they gained the brutal reward of the *bastinado*, while others received the torture of the wheel. Assembling was not the only reason that Protestants were sent to the galleys. In the records kept by a visiting doctor, Henri Bertrand, one reads that the penalty of the galleys could be imposed for resisting the dragoons, attempted flight abroad, or for helping fugitives, the possession of arms, recanting one's abjuration as well as "keeping pious frequentations." A few ministers, like Matthieu Leblanchon from Suesgres near Mérindol who was supposed to die in Grenoble, were paroled to the galleys[22]

In the process of moving towards the galleys, the Huguenots were often immured in dark, fetid, and lice-infested prisons. Here is the experience of Elie Neau, who was sent to the Chateau d'If:

> I was put on the 20th of May 1696, in a subterranean hole; wherein I remained till the 1st of July following. The place was so disposed that we were obliged to go down a ladder into a dry ditch, and then go up the same ladder into an old tower, through a cannon-hole. The vault or arch wherein we were put, was as dark as if there had been no manner of light in heaven; stinking; and so miserably dirty that I verily believe there is not a more miserable place in the world. All our senses were attacked at once. Sight, by darkness; Taste, by hunger; Smell, by the stench of the place; Seeing, by lice and other vermin; and Hearing by the horrid blasphemies and cursing, which the soldiers, who were obliged to bring us victuals, vomited against God and our holy religion.[23]

The Huguenot, Daniel Serres, had a similar experience. Already suffering in his lungs, he was immured in an excessively damp cell. The physician refused to give him any help. Even worse, when the physician was informed by Serres that his mouth had hurt him so much that he had pulled out five or six of his teeth, he replied: "If you want to stay healthier in the dungeon, you should not only lose the rest of your teeth, but also your brains." The unhappy man wrote: "What greater misery can one imagine than that of being deprived of the light of day during entire years, being delivered a prey to the avarice and severity of a keeper, and to feel dying at every moment?"[24]

The fate of the women led them to convents or to prisons. Madame du Ry for instance, the wife of a famous Parisian architect, and her daughters were taken to the convent of the Ursulines in Paris and kept in isolation. Madame la Baronne d'Aigaliers, who tried to escape with her children, was caught around Montpellier and locked into the convent of St. Ursula. Some of these women made such a nuisance of themselves, by doggedly trying to propagate the Protestant faith within the convent that they were deported. Others died in the faith, like Marguerite de Beringhen de la Luzerne, who expired at eighty in the Convent of the Visitation in Caen.[25]

Some were sent to various prisons. For instance, Madame Mouret, the sister of Madame d'Aigaliers, the wife of the Baron, was imprisoned first at Pons and then at Pézunas.[26] The most famous prison was the Tour de Constance at the sinisterly named town of Aigues-Mortes. The only escape was death or pardon. The prisoners' heads were shaved. Antoine Court, a famous regenerator of the French Protestant Church, made it a point of honor to visit the Tour of Constance. He was appalled at what he saw, and thus he reported the scene: "Two or three poor women or girls left in this tower for many years, abandoned by the entire world, left as prey for vermin, destitute of clothes, resembling skeletons."[27] Among those immured were Anne Gaussainte, who died after thirty-nine years of captivity, blind Marie Béreaud who was in the tower for twenty-four years, Jacquette Vigne who endured nineteen years there, and Marguerite Anglivielle who at seventy-five died there after thirteen years.[28] The most renowned of them all was Marie Durand who entered the Tour at fifteen and left thirty-eight years later. She kept the hope of the rest of the company alive, through her moral and spiritual courage. She is believed to have inscribed on the wall the famous word " RESISTEZ."[29]

The sufferings of the long march to the galleys in chain gangs from the various prisons of France are recorded by one who had to march from Dunkirk to Marseilles, Marteilhe. His march took six months, and he insisted that it caused him more suffering than the following twelve years in the galleys. The first glimpse he had of the manacled galley slaves was horrifying. Each carried heavy iron collars and a short chain, which linked captives in twos. These chains were not removed at night, making it impossible to find a comfortable posture in which to sleep. Marteilhe tells of the cruelties of one moonless night en route. The convicts were made to take off their chains and all their clothes and to march for two foul hours in the bitter cold, while their tormentors examined their possessions to see if they had files or knives they might use to cut their chains. In Marteilhe's own words:

> It is easy to guess whether any money they found escaped from these harpies. They grabbed all they could use . . . And when the unhappy men asked them what they had taken from them, they were rewarded by blows from their muskets or their staffs.

Then the chain was ordered back to where they had left their clothes. He continues:

> But, O cruel spectacle! most of the unhappy group was so stiff from the frost we had suffered that it was impossible for us to march back to the place where we had left our clothing. It was then that the blows of batons and whips fell, and that this horrible treatment could animate these poor bodies, all frozen, and some lying stiff and dead, and others dying, the barbarous men of the watch dragged them by the chin on their necks like carrion, their bodies streaming with blood from the blows they had received. That night, or the next morning, 18 were dead.[30]

How painful the march to the galleys was is confirmed by the experience of Louis de Marolles, former adviser to King Louis XIV, who was imprisoned in Des Tournelles in 1686, awaiting the transportation to the galleys of Marseilles. He wrote:

> 53 men of us were sleeping in a place of approximately 5 meters long and not one was larger than a meter and a half. On my right was a sick peasant, whose head was at my feet and his feet at my head. It was the same with the others. There wasn't one of us who did not envy the conditions of many dogs and horses. Altogether there were 95 condemned persons, but two of them died on that day; we still have 14 or 15 sick persons, and there are few better than that."[31]

Galleys were eventually located at Marseilles, Toulon and Dunkirk. From 1692 to 1702 there were several new galleys, two each for Brest, Bordeaux and Saint-Malo, nine for Marseilles, and six for Dunkirk. The galley slaves wore a red cassock, a red shirt and pants, and their heads were shaved in order to prevent vermin infestation.

The general constituency of the galleys was composed of deserters, criminals, debtors, Turks, and Protestants. The Huguenots condemned to the galleys had often attempted flight abroad, attended a religious gathering, or housed a pastor. They were condemned without consideration of rank, age, or health. As to their total numbers, Gaston Tournier states that two thousand is a reasonable figure.[32]

To understand the difficulties for the galley slaves, one must imagine the conditions in which they worked, pulling days in and days out on the oars and suffering endless irritation from fleas and lice. The Protestants endured spiritual suffering caused by the demand that they raise their hats as the procession of the Mass passes and by the obligation to kneel as the Mass was said. This required insincerity on their part. Marteilhe reports that the worst persecutor was Major-General Bombelle who said "Kneel, dog, and if you cannot pray to God in this posture, pray to the Devil"[33]

Other moral suffering was the destruction of letters by family or friends. Moreover it was only Protestant men on the galleys who could not receive family visits; nor could they go unchained or unsupervised to sell trinkets in ports for profit. In addition they were frightened of capture by pirates to be sold as slaves at Algiers.[34]

One of the best descriptions was provided by Admiral Baudin in a letter he sent to the president of the Historical Society of French Protestantism.[35]

> The galley-slaves were chained two and two upon the benches of the galleys, and were there employed in plying the long and heavy oars . . . Along the center of the keel of each galley, and in the mid-space between the benches of the rowers ran a kind of gallery called the *'coursive'*, upon which continually paraded the overseers known by the name of *comes*, each one armed with a bull's pizzle, with which he lashed the shoulders of the wretches, who, in his opinion did not row with sufficient strength. The galley-slaves passed their lives upon their benches; they ate and slept thereon, without being able to change their position more than the length of their chains permitted, and having no other shelter from the rain, the heat of the sun, or the chill of night, than a cloth which was extended above their bench, when the galley was not under way, and the wind was not too violent.

One only need add that five hundred oarsmen were required for one royal galley, which was fifty yards long and forty feet wide. There were fifty banks of rowers; twenty-five on each side. Each oar was served by six convicts, who were bound to their benches by a chain riveted to one of their legs. The working of the lengthy oars was exhausting, and at any sign of weakness in a galley slave, his back was struck with a rope or a *bastinade*.

Those in the galleys included several aristocrats, such as Louis de Marolles, former counselor to the king, the Baron of Montbeton, parent of the Duke of La Force, the Baron of Salgas, the Sieurs of Lasterne, of La Continge and of L'Aubonnière, and such heroic men as Elie Neau, Sabatier, and the three brothers Serres. On a list of 105 galley slaves for the faith provided by Antoine Court, could be found two Chevaliers de Saint Louis and forty-six gentilshommes. Most surprising of all, Admiral Baudin found evidence of a thirteen-year-old boy included among the galley slaves.[36] These men of culture had to live without privacy or comfort and were goaded by the curses and gibes of their criminal companions. No wonder they seemed to be floating hells to the Huguenots. As Ruben Saillens puts it: "death on the scaffold would have been a lighter sentence than this slow dying."[37]

The heroic Jean Fabre, who substituted himself for his seventy-eight-year-old father, caught at the same illicit religious meeting, was horrified when he caught the first glimpse of his galley. He wrote:

> Until then, I acknowledge my firmness had not undergone the least alteration; this happened only when I had to enter in the fatal vessel, and I was myself unclothed to put on the ignominious uniform of the scoundrels also living there, confounded with what was vilest on earth, chained with one of them, and thrown on the same form, then my heart failed. I fell into a fit, what trouble they had to revive me, and then my hair was cut, the terrible sign of the most frightened slavery. A torrent of tears flooded my personality. One of these unhappy persons, followed by a guard, brought me in a wooden bowl, cooked only in water, a black loaf, the regular food of these unfortunates. It was put beside me. I did not want it at all, preferring a thousand times death, and resolved to let myself die of hunger . . . On this first night I let myself think of my misery beneath a lamp suspended in the middle of the galley, where my eyes surveyed the beings that surrounded me, covered with rags and vermin which tormented them. I imagined myself in a hell which the remorse of crime tormented unceasingly, and in a gloomy silence my eyes stopped on myself. My conscience did not reproach me, my soul was calm; my chain did not weigh on my spirit, but only on my body. I raised it to relieve myself and then I let it drop.[38]

The other shattering experience in the galleys was to be present when the *bastinado* or a heavy cane was used, usually when a man would not take off his hat or bow at the passing of the Host of the Eucharist. The chaplains aboard often initiated it. The great exception was Jean Bion, a Catholic, who was assailed by terrible doubts as an official aboard a galley. Could he continue to belong to a religion which professed charity, but practiced violence of the most virulent kind? These Huguenots, he thought, in their resignation to the will of God, their firmness in faith, and their patience in suffering, were they not more truly Christian than their oppressors? Bion's conclusion was: "Finally their wounds were so many mouths which announced the Reformed religion to me, and their blood was the semen of regeneration."[39]

The horrific example of the Huguenot Sabatier's treatment for a different offense should be recalled. In 1717, a letter, which he had written to one of his sick friends on a galley, enclosing a small sum from a charity, was opened and brought to the attention of the intendant De Montfort. The latter demanded of Sabatier who had given him this money, but Sabatier excused himself from providing this information. He was then maltreated with many blows of heavy cane, and seeing that he would rather die than bring prejudice against those who were generous, asked him from time to time if Sabatier would answer, but he said nothing. De

Montfort had him stripped naked, placed his belly on the ground and had him battered by two Turks. But he did not utter any cry. He continued to remain silent. Then the Intendant pushed him with his foot upright and in this position ordered the slaves to beat him. However, as Sabatier still remained silent, de Montfort said to the clerk that was present, "See what a devil of a religion this is!" Then he had this unhappy man placed again with his belly on the ground and had him beaten four times more. The Intendant said to him: "Doesn't the King nourish you?" To which Sabatier replied: "If we had to live on what the King gives us, we should soon all be dead. But if you should learn of those who help us, you would make them suffer thoroughly." After all this, they put a band over his eyes and threw him into a dungeon, where he remained with the heavy chains and had only the bread and water of the galley.[40]

The threat of being sent to the New World was even more frightful to the Huguenots. There were, indeed, reports of shipwrecks off the coast of Martinique or Saint Domingo in which very few survived, which fed the fear that Huguenots were embarked on vessels in order to be drowned. A letter from Cadiz by a Cévenol in the month of April 1687 shows that they feared being sold as slaves in America. "One sends them to the islands of America to be sold to the highest offer."[41]

A single drawing of 1686 whose title in translation reads, "sure and honest means of bringing back heretics to the Catholic faith" exhibits ironically the various means used to "persuade" Protestants to renounce their faith and convert to the faith of their oppressors. A kneeling figure, presumably a towering De Marillac, an Intendant renowned for his cruelty in dragooning, threatens a Huguenot, while surrounded by the instruments of torture—a prison, a galley, a gallows, a fire, and the ominous wheel.[42]

Of tortures applied to single individuals probably the most feared was death at the wheel. The victim's legs and arms were broken and he was then placed on a wheel, which was mercilessly whirled round, and round, until the centrifugal pressure forced the blood to flood through his broken extremities. One minister was bound to the wheel and broken alive because he tried to inform all Protestant lands abroad about the suffering of French Protestants. He had written " when God permits pastors to be put to death for the Gospel, they preach more loudly and more effectually in the grave than they did in their lifetime and, meanwhile, God does not fail to raise up other laborers for the harvest."[43]

Still some believed that the bitterness caused by the *bastinade* in the galleys was worse than the torture at the wheel. The following letter confirms this judgment:

> The Wheel, on which the Martyrs of our blessed Lord formerly expired, was very sweet, if compared with the bitterness of our sufferings; because their torments proceeded without intermission till Death gave them the crown of Martyrdom. But our punishment which pierces into the very bones; which bruises, which tears, the skin off to the very blood; which makes all the back swell with the multitude of blows, given with a rope done over with pitch and tar, and dipped half a foot into the sea; and which leaves a man half-dead, by reason of One and Twenty blows given at one beating by a lusty Turk; who leaves us in that wretched condition, in order to begin again, in the afternoon, or the next morning, as fiercely and as cruelly as ever; permitting these miserable men *to live thus*, that this barbarous usage may be the more lasting; and that they may put naked again upon the Coursey (*Gangway*).[44]

Another brutal form of murder was by burning—the death usually reserved to heretics and witches. This was the fate of a sixty-six-year-old man named Guizot who fell sick out of remorse for having been forced to abjure his faith as a Protestant. Foreseeing his impending death, he retracted his abjuration in front of a vicar who had come to give him the Last Rites and bring him Communion. He refused both. The vicar forced the host into his mouth and Guizot spat it out. Pursued as sacrilegious, he was condemned to be burnt. He died with the courage of a martyr.[45]

The heroism of the martyrs facing such an agonizing death as burning was bound to have a powerful impact on bystanders. Such was the death of Ann Audebert, being surrounded by a circle of flame, and crying out: "My God! The beautiful cincture which my Husband gives me!" Jean Ecrivain, who died in similar circumstances at Lyon is reported as feeling:

> If we consider the infinite glory and the immortal crown prepared for us above in heaven, even in the middle of death. Then shall we see our Heavenly Father clearly face-to-face and know Him as He knows us, who shall wipe away the tears of all His children, whom He will crown with glory and immortalize to live with Him forever."[46]

One of the bravest of the martyrs, who died by hanging, was Claude Brousson. He was the great defender of French Protestants in Holland and Germany who returned to preach passionately in France, despite the dangers. Caught finally in France, he was taken a prisoner to Montpellier. Having arrived at the Place de Pérou, and wishing to address the crowd, his words were silenced by eighteen drummers. First, he faced the wheel; then, the rope on which he hung broke at the first twist of the pulley. The priest accompanying him tried to persuade Brousson that this was a providential accident that would give him time to convert to Catholicism before his death. Brousson replied: "May almighty God reward you for your great charity towards me and may He give us the grace to enable both of us to see His face in paradise."[47]

Huguenots who remained faithful to their religion had few alternatives if discovered—all of which were painful. Pastors expected the worst, mainly hanging. In summation, George A. Rothrock writes:

> "Manhunts dug out pastors who tried to hide rather than leave and generally they were hanged with little ceremony. Secret congregations were uncovered, and when they were found, troops were ordered to fire into the unarmed crowd. Surviving males were sent to the living hell of the king's galleys, women to the prisons—only a little less terrible, and children to Catholic orphanages."[48]

When one considers all that the Huguenots suffered, as individuals or as a group, in the cruellest forms of persecution, one would wish to apply to those who retained their Protestant faith these words directed to the faithful in the galleys: "Il semble que toute vertu s'y fut réfugiée! Obscur ailleurs, là Dieu était visible."[49]

Notes

1. Reported from King, ed, *The Life and Letters of John Locke* in *B.S.H.P.F.*, vol. 58, 417–21.

2. See Patrice Jacquelot de Chantemerle de Vilette, *Les Jacquelot Protestants du XVIè au XVIIIè siècle en Champagne et dans les pays étrangers*, (Paris: chez l'auteur, 1994.)

3. For instance, Madame de Voulat, who was imprisoned in the fortress of Blaye near Bordeaux. South Carolina Historical Society. Crottet Mss. 31.

4. Poole, R.L. *A History of the Huguenots of the Dispersion at the recall of the Edict of Nantes*, (London: Macmillan, 1880), 13.

5. Charles Baird, *The History of the Huguenot Emigration to America*. (New York: Dodd, Mead and Co., 1885), vol. 1, 6.

6. Jean Orcibal, *Louis XIV et les Protestants*, (Paris: Vrin, 1951), indicates that the fund came from one-third of the revenues of Saint. Germain and Cluny Abbeys which the king allowed to remain without a leader for a while in order to obtain their revenues. Pope Innocent I, Bossuet, Fénelon, and Bourdaloue, all approved the program.

7. Newport J. D. White, "Gleanings from the correspondance of a great Huguenot. Elie Bouhéreau of La Rochelle." *P.H.S.L.*, vol. 9, n. 2. Elie Richard seems to have been also an inventor of repute, as he was allowed to die in peace at La Rochelle.

8. This comprehensive catalogue comes from Charles Baird, *Huguenot Emigration*, vol. 1, 249.

9. "Curieuse lettre de François Fargues, dit Tristan, réfugié en Angleterre, à Bonaventure Dehoue, prêtre du Mas-d'Azil. 1748" *B.S.H.P.F.*, vol. 46, 260–274.

10. R. Zuber, and L. Theis, eds., *La Révocation de l'Edit de Nantes et le Protestantisme français en 1686*, (Paris: Société de l'Histoire du Protestantisme français: 1986), 64.

11. Even Intendant Baville acknowledged that this was the case, when he said: "The new converts will confess and have communion as much as we want, in order not to be pressurized and threatened by secular powers; but this only produces sacrileges; one must attack the hearts, that's where religion is seated, and one cannot establish it solidly without winning their hearts." Fonds Mortemart, n. 100. quoted by Jules Chavannes, in "Essai sur les abjurations parmi les Réformes de France sous le règne de Louis XIV" *B.S.H.P.F.*, vol. 21, 201–207 and 205.

12. A translation of Claude's famous *Complainte* entitled *An account of the Persecutions and Oppressions of the Protestants in France*. (Cologne: Pierre Marteau, 1686), 19–20.

Persecution: The Necessity to Escape

13. *The story of the Huguenots*, (Cambridge, U.S.: Cambridge University Press, 1920), 45

14. De Janzé, *Les Huguenots: Cent Ans de Persecution*, 220f. See also the testimony of the Sieur Poysal, public prosecutor at La Rochelle, who shows that Monsieur de Demiun, who had no soldiers under his command, managed to form a troop composed of the archers of the navy and of the mounted constables to which he added a Jesuit priest, a former judge, and a few more people in order to participate creatively in the missionary work. He had the Jesuit preach them a sermon before he proceeded by force. Found in South Carolina Historical Society: Crottet Mss. 14, 157–158.

15. De Janzé, *Les Huguenots*, 230.

16. De Janzé, *Les Huguenots*, 232 f.

17. *BHPF*, vol. 22, 452–471.

18. Bernard Cotteret, *The Huguenots in England; Immigration and Settlement c. 1550–1700*. (Cambridge: Cambridge University Press, 1991), 279–280, using the Rawlinson MSS. C 954 fol. in the Bodleian Library, Oxford University.

19. This was called the "supplice de la claie," which spared no one. For instance, a former Counsellor of the Court is dragged this way in Toulouse on November 28, 1686, or the wife of a doctor from Montpellier, Dame Carquet. At Metz, Suzanne Gentilhomme is dragged and her head hits the pavement . . . See. *B.H.S.P.F.*, vol. 52, 385–97.

20. See South Carolina Historical Society. Crottet Mss. Vol. 14, 285–86.

21. Delation was paid handsomely. In *Complainte par un Protestant exilé en Angleterre sur la surprise d'une Assemblée tenue au Désert près de Nîmes.*1720. The informer who went to tell the governor that an assembly was taking place was paid forty *pistoles*. See in South Carolina Historical Society: Crottet Mss. n. 44.

22. Crottet Mss. 37: the copy of a manuscript which was deposited in the Archives of the French Mint of Yverson and which contains a story of the city of Yverson.

23. Arber, Edward, ed. *The torments of Protestant Slaves in the French King's Galleys and in the dungeons of Marseilles, 1686–1707 A. D.* (London: Privately printed, 1907), 189.

24. De Janzé, *Les Huguenots*, 165.

25. "Une famille d'architectes parisiens, les Du Ry, expulsés par la Révocation de l'Edit de Nantes" *B.S.H.P.F.*, vol. 45, 523–530.

26. Mme la Baronne de Charmisay, *Un gentilhomme huguenot au temps des Camisards. Le Baron d'Aigaliers*, (Le Mas Soubeyran: Musée du Désert, 1935.)

27. Court, Antoine. *A faithful Account of the Cruelties done to the Protestants*, (London: Nutt, 1700), quoted by G. E. Falguerolles in "Les prisonnières de la Tour de Constance" *B.S.H.P.F.*, vol. 116, 383.

28. See the article by G.E. de Falguerolles in the *BHSPF*, vol. 116 and S. Mours, *Les églises Reformées en France*. (Paris and Strasbourg: Librairie Protestante, 1955), 17.

29. *BSHPF*, vol. 116.

30. Athanase Cocquerel, *Les forçats pour la Foi; étude historique, 1684–1775*, (Paris: M. Lévy, 1886) 49–62.

31. De Janzé, *Cent ans de Persécution*, 178 ff.

32. G. Tournier, *Les Galères de France et les galériens Protestants des XVIIè et du XVIIIè siècles* (Mas Soubeyran: Musée du Désert, 1943), 61.

33. "Règlements faits sur les galères de France par les Confesseurs qui souffrent pour la Vérité de l'Evangile" *B.S.H.P.F.* vol. 17, 25, note 1 which cites Marteilhe, *Mémoires*, 346–47.

34. See " Deux lettres de Protestants captifs à Alger de 1687" *B.H.S.P.F.*, vol. 110, 54 ff.

35. It appears in *B.H.S.F.P.*, June–July 1852, 53.

36. De Janzé, *Les Huguenots*, 195ff.

37. Ruben Saillens, *The Soul of France*, (London: morgan and Scott, 1916), 66.

38. Coquerel, *Les forçats pour la Foi*, 201ff.

39. Pierre M. Conlon, *Jean-Francois Bion et sa relation des Tourments qu'on fait souffrir aux Protestants qui sont sur les Galères de France*, (Genève: Droz, 1966), 112. Another proselyte in the galley was Jean Fayan de Bordeaux who, in 1694, declared to the *aumonier* on board that, although he was born a Catholic, he wished to live and die a Protestant. Asked by the bishop why he could not longer live a Catholic, he replied: because of "Purgatory, calling upon the saints, the adoration of pictures and the real presence of Christ in the Eucharist". *B.S.H.P.F.*, vol. 17, 338–42.

40. *Lettres historiques concernant ce qui se passe de plus important en Europe*, (The Hague: Sept. 1707), 311–14; also in *Bulletin of the Huguenot Society of London*, vol. 21, 151–52.

41. Reported by Elie Benoit and quoted by De Janzé, *The Huguenots*, 152–54.

42. This drawing turned into a lithograph, appears in Tessa Murdoch, ed. *The Quiet Conquest. The Huguenots*. (London: Museum of London, 1985).

43. H. M. Baird, *The Huguenots and the Revocation of the Edict of Nantes*, vol. 2, 210.

44. *B.S.H.P.F.*, vol. 116.

45. De Janzé, *Les Huguenots*, 99.

46. Emile G. Léonard, *Le Protestant Français*, (Paris: P.U.F, 1955), 29.

47. Eugène and Emile Haag, *La France Protestante*, (Paris: Fischbacher, 1877), vol 3, 258.

48. George A. Rothrock, *The Huguenots: A Biography of a Minority*. (Chicago: Nelson Hall, 1979), 176.

49. J. Michelet, *Louis XIV et la Révocation de l'Edit de Nantes*, (Paris: Flammarion, 1898-99), 337. A translation would read "It seems as if all courage had taken refuge there! Obscure elsewhere, God was visible there!"

Chapter 3

Ways of Escape from France

Having shaken the dust of the tyrannous land of France from their feet, Huguenots turned their faces to the promised lands. Although there are lists of emigrants in various parts of Europe and in legal documents from America, some of which indicate the provenance of the refugees, there is still a question of their total numbers, as well as the exact locations from which they escaped. Thus, this chapter will inevitably provide near approximations or shadows of the reality of escaping from the realm. Accounts of the modes of escape, and their sufferings on the way are, however, abundant, owing to the high level of literacy among those who escaped and their desire to keep letters as records of their ordeal. Therefore a fairly good record exists of the attraction provided by the lands to which they fled, as well as of the dangers of their flight.

As to numbers, nineteenth century historians appear to have exaggerated the number of Protestant emigrants. Charles Weiss, for example, thought that the total in the seventeenth century was about four hundred thousand, while Reginald Lane Poole reduced the numbers to about three hundred thousand, and assigned the exiles as follows: one hundred thousand to Holland; eighty thousand to England, Ireland and America; twenty-five thousand to Switzerland; and seventy-five thousand to Germany.[1] One of the most careful modern "guesstimates" is that of Robin Gwynne. He claims that the proper number of exiles is as follows: ten thousand to America; ten thousand to Ireland; twenty thousand to Denmark and northeast Europe; forty to fifty thousand to England; to the Dutch Republic fifty to sixty thousand; to Germany, twenty-five to thirty thousand; to Switzerland twenty-two thousand; and to the Cape of Good Hope, four hundred.[2]

The primary attraction of the chosen countries was, of course, liberty of conscience—to live in a Protestant land where they would be able to worship God in their accustomed way. Switzerland, Britain, Holland, Germany, Norway, most of North America, and South Africa proved so inviting.

Among the possible attractions to a country are curiosity and proximity. In normal circumstances curiosity would be a natural magnet drawing folk to the new lands, but in the situation of dreadful desperation dogging the footsteps of the Huguenots, it would be their last consideration. Because of the danger of being caught by one of the king's guards en route, it was also important to select a country of refuge as close as possible to the place in France in which the would-be emigrants lived. In all parts of their journey, they were surrounded by a large majority of Catholic spies who, if they brought the Protestants to justice, would gain the right to half their property and would be taxless for twelve years. In such a situation, nearness, after the assurance of a safe haven, would be a prime consideration. The risk of getting caught was not limited to the escape from France but extended to subsequent travel. Daniel Borel B. Valence from Dauphiné, for instance, had remained in Amsterdam for two years, and was on a ship bound for the Indies when it was caught at Saint Malo in 1689.[3]

Which parts of Europe, then offered proximity to France as their allure, and which parts of France chose particular countries? For those who inhabited the eastern side of France, Switzerland (especially, the Protestant cantons of Lausanne and Berne) and particularly the city of Geneva, would be the first choice, because of proximity and the use of the same language. Geneva's attractions were three: it was French speaking, honored as the Holy City of Calvinists, and conveniently close to north eastern France. Geneva, however, was a small city, had limited accommodation and job openings, and was stretched to the uttermost. For the decade after the Revocation, it found a permanent home for three thousand French refugees, and it provided temporary hospitality for all on their way to Holland or Germany. Those who lived in northern France would be drawn to either Holland or England, possibly via the French-speaking Channel Islands of Jersey or Guernsey. Those in French ports would be attracted to Dutch or English ports, such as Amsterdam, London, Dover, Plymouth, Southampton, or Rye.

Using the figures and locations of Samuel Mours, exiles from the Ile de France, Picardy, and Champagne, who were 43 percent of the Huguenots of that region, probably selected Holland, as well as the 26 percent from Berry and Orleanais. The 36 percent of the Protestants from Normandy who had become refugees by 1690 and the 58 percent of those from Britanny are likely to have chosen England or Holland; similarly, the 58 percent of Huguenot refugees from Anjou, Touraine, or Maine; from there, some would leave for North America. The 20 percent from Poitou and the 26 percent from Aunis and Saintonge as well as the 10 percent from Languedoc and Guyenne would probably also choose Holland or England.[4] Some of the latter, and most of the exiles from the Cévennes, might prefer Switzerland. Residents from Dauphiné, and from Provence, who formed 25 percent and 17 percent of the Huguenots, respectively, would naturally choose Switzerland and might well continue into Germany. The highest percentage of the Huguenots to select exile (59 percent)—those from Bordeaux—were likely to emigrate to America, England or Holland. Our figures for the percentages of the exiled Huguenots of an area are almost exact, but the places they selected are largely guesswork. They might have to move from their initial choice of country, as overpopulation strained its resources.

Indeed, the likelihood of finding suitable employment, or, at least, charity in the country of adoption weighed heavily in their decision. In France, according to Charles Baird: "The policy of restriction bearing upon the family, the school and the Church, also limited the Huguenots' daily profession or calling."[5] In their new surroundings, Huguenots needed to adapt to the country's needs, as it needed to adapt to the new refugees' talents and needs. In such circumstances, the probability of foreign employment was a primary consideration for emigration. Because South Africa and America provided good possibilities for the Huguenot peasants of France, some were willing to venture to these distant lands.

Another important factor in attracting French refugees was that their predecessors had found security in a particular land they were considering as their haven. Reassurance was especially heartening for those facing a dangerous and difficult excursion into a foreign country. This reassurance was provided by the historical welcome that England had given to French-speaking Walloons and the French generally, for over a hundred years. French emigrants had found shelter several times before in England. In 1550, King Edward VI, by patent royal, entrusted John A. Lasco as superintendant of all the Protestant refugees from France, Holland, Germany and Switzerland. Shortly afterward, the French gained the chapel for their use in Threadneedle Street in London, where they could worship in their own tongue. In 1548, this church had four hundred and fifty communicants. Queen Elizabeth had encouraged French Protestant settlements. In the seventeenth century, the minutes of the consistory of the French Church in London show that sixteen people made their reconnaissance in 1685; 274 during the year after the Revocation; 2,237 in 1687, after James II had broken with the Tories and issued the Declaration of Indulgence, granting toleration to dissenters; and 500 in 1688, after which the numbers decline once again.[6]

The Church for Walloons was founded in 1561 in Canterbury. A large number of Huguenots was added, so that by 1634 it had become a community of nine hundred. Other French churches were founded at Norwich in 1554 and one at Sandwich for French refugees previously located in London and Norwich. Even before the Revocation of the Edict of Nantes in 1685, other French churches had been established in London, at the Savoy, Marylebone, and Castle Street, and, after 1688, there were twenty-seven new foundations for a multitude of worshippers. All this, which was widely known, must have induced many hesitant French refugees to choose that land, especially if they had relatives or friends in Britain.

The Dutch had also proved a haven to Protestants: they had come from England under Mary the Catholic and as Puritans under Elizabeth. They had also come from other lands. It generously provided room and board for the French exiled laity, and excused them from taxation for twelve years.[7]

Some lands were even eager to attract immigrants and advertised the advantages to be found in coming to them. This was certainly the case in both Ireland and South Carolina; the English government encouraged such settlements.[8] Brothers then went to seek their fortune in different lands—for instance, Stephen Mazyk, who went to Ireland, and his brother Isaac Mazyk, who prospered in South Carolina.

In Ireland, King William III invited, for instance, Louis Crommelin, who had escaped to Holland, to be the overseer of the linen trade. Crommelin made his headquarters at Lisburne in the county of Antrim. He brought one thousand looms from Holland and brought several Huguenots like himself to found a colony there. He also directed another venture to create the manufacture of hempen sailcloth, with plants in Rathkeale and Cork, Waterford, and Rathbridge in Kildare.[9] This productive Huguenot gave employment to hundreds of fellow believers and contributed to the wealth of Ireland.

The most notable and generous invitation came from Germany, inititated by Frederick William, king of Prussia and Elector of Brandenburg. To attract French Huguenots, he treated them as if they were already colonists—he assisted their travel expenses, provided houses and churches for them, allowed them to conduct their law-courts in the French language, and even initially excused them from most taxes. The French had their own ecclesiastical consistories as well as synods and were made to feel so much at home that De Janzé does not exaggerate when he states that: "it seemed to them that they still lived among their parents and friends . . ."[10]

England, as it had been in the past, was generous to the French immigrants in two ways—through both charitable collections and government grants of the status of either denizen or, even better, naturalization. The latter conferred both trade privileges and rights of inheritance. The insistence that every English Church should contribute charitable collections for the exiles was stressed in the moving appeal of Henry Compton, Bishop of London, which included the following words in print:

> You have such an object of charity before you, as it may be, no case could more deserve your pity. It is not a flight to save their lives, but what is a thousand times more dear, their consciences. They are not fled by permission (except the ministers who are banished) but with the greatest difficulty and hardship imaginable. And therefore it will be an act of the highest compassion to comfort and relieve them."[11]

A series of briefs, ordering parish collections for Protestant refugees was issued between 1681 and 1694, which produced a total of ninety thousand pounds. Between 1689 and 1693, the civil list of William and Mary—the Royal Bounty—added another thirty-nine thousand pounds.[12] In addition, the relevant committee of the French churches in London reported that weekly assistance was given to 15,500 refugees in 1678 and to 27,000 refugees in 1687.[13]

Holland, besides the privileges already mentioned, also created several establishments for women. Prince William of Orange, like the King of Prussia, was eager to attract soldiers trained by Turenne to his country, whom he later used to defeat the armies of France. Huguenots also relieved Holland's shortness of ministers; French pastors filled in professional appointments in its universities and in leading congregations in such cities as Amsterdam, La Haye and Leyden. Finally, the Dutch also provided 400 Huguenots with the possibility of settling in South Africa around the Cape of Good Hope in order to establish vineyards at The Paarl.

On the American continent, the history of rivalry between the French and the English created a split in reactions. Canada, as of 1633, was closed to the Huguenots, except for trade with La Rochelle. In 1676, the "Conseil Supérieur" of Québec specified that Protestants could not assemble for worship although they were permitted to come to Canada during the summer. Some of them came regardless, much to the chagrin of the Bishop, who obtained from the Ministry of the Navy the assurance, in 1683, that none of them could settle in Canada or in Acadia.[14] Few Huguenots, therefore, went to Canada: still, in 1671, the colony of Port-Royal welcomed sixty refugees. Chinard, in his analysis, passes judgment on the kings of France who missed, according to him, a great opportunity to have a loyal and prosperous colony and solve the religious split in France.[15]

Some Protestants reached the Antilles. The religious laws that governed France, however, also governed the Antilles in St. Kitts, Guadeloupe, and Martinique. Although some of the governors closed their eyes, the Huguenots could not openly practice their religion; which caused a number of people from the Antilles to end up in Charleston or elsewhere after 1668 and particularly in 1686.[16]

Boston kept frequent links with La Rochelle and with the Antilles, which is why, as early as 1662, Jean Touton asked whether a contingent of Huguenots might come to Boston; this was approved August 16, 1662. Increase Mather, briefed by Nathaniel Mather from Ireland, kept the Protestants of Boston aware of the persecutions occurring in France through his 1682 sermon, *The Church a subject of persecution. Fast sermon on the persecution of the Protestants in France*. Thomas Cobbet of Ipswich congratulated him for having a day of prayer and mortification in his church in sympathy with the French Protestants. Yet, suspicion toward the French remained because of the Bostonians' awareness of the historical background of the former wars between England and France in nearby Canada.

The settlement around the New York area was affected by the rivalry between the French, the English, and the Dutch who wanted Frenchmen to cultivate the land. Huguenot refugees are mentioned as early as 1660, around which time the persecuted Vaudois reached Delaware and New Amsterdam. Other Huguenots from other areas of France arrived in the following years, most of them agricultural hands. After the Revocation they did not usually come directly from France, but via England or Holland.

The settlements of New Rochelle and New Paltz came after the Revocation. The former, founded around 1688, grew until a church was built in 1710. But the settlers were too closed in upon themselves. Therefore, it disappeared around 1738 when the minister Bondet was replaced by an Anglican minister. The colony of New Paltz seems to have been formed by settlers who came from the Palatinate and maintained close links to the Dutch Church.

Delaware, Virginia, and the Carolinas wanted the French for a definite purpose—the cultivation of the vine and the mulberry. It seems that the

Huguenots did best in South Carolina, where they eventually cultivated indigo and rice. The warm climate and the swamps were propitious for the production of rice. The French would particularly enjoy the vast acreage available for minimal payment as well as the ability to bring in black Barbadians to help cultivate the land.[17] Rice attracted ships to Charleston and Georgetown. Rice money paid for the construction of fine houses in both centers, and for the education of the sons of planters sent to Oxford and Cambridge to become statesmen, physicians, surgeons, and scientists.[18] Seven churches were founded. Of those, one still flourishes today.

Travellers of our own century require much imagination to evaluate the ingenuity and courage needed by the Huguenot emigrants of the seventeenth and eighteenth centuries. Elie Benoit writes vividly of the ingenious modes of escape:

> Of those who lived near the sea board, some would conceal themselves in bales of merchandise or under loads of charcoal, or in empty hogsheads. Others were stowed in the holds of vessels, where they lay in heaps, men, women and children, coming forth only in the dead of night to breathe their air. Some would risk themselves in frail barks, for a voyage the very thought of which would once have made them shudder with fear. The guards placed by the king to watch the coast, sometimes became softened, and found such opportunities of gain in favoring the flight of Protestants, that they even went so far as to assist them. The captains of cruisers, who had orders to intercept any vessel that might carry fugitives, themselves carried great numbers of them out of the kingdom: and in almost every seaport, some admiralty officers, tempted by the profits which the shipmasters shared with them, allowed many persons to pass whose hiding places they would not have found it difficult to discover. There were families that paid from six to eight thousand *livres* for their escape. The same thing happened on the landward side of the kingdom. Persons stationed to guard roads and passages would furnish guides at a certain price to those whom they had been instructed to arrest, and would even serve in that capacity themselves. As for such as could not avail themselves of these advantages, for want of skills or lack of means, they contrived a thousand ways to elude the vigilance of the countless sentinels appointed to prevent their flight. Often they disguised themselves as peasants, driving cattle before them, or carrying bundles as if on their way to some markets; or as soldiers, returning to their garrison in some town of Holland or Germany."[19]

Unwealthy Huguenots used even greater imagination to trick the royal guards. Charles Baird reports:

> They travelled by night only; they crossed rivers by fords scarcely known or unused because of danger; they spent the day in forests and in caverns or concealed in barns or haystacks. Women resorted to the same artifices as men, and fled under all sorts of disguises. They dressed themselves as servants, as peasants, as nurses. They trundled wheelbarrows. They carried hods, they bore burdens. They

passed themselves off as the wives of their guides. They dressed in men's clothes and followed on foot as lackeys, while their guides rode on horseback as persons of quality. Men and women disguised themselves as mendicants, and passed through the places where they were most exposed to suspicion in tattered garments, begging their bread from door to door.[20]

The characters they invented for themselves were a tribute to their ingenuity. They might appear to be pilgrims en route to holy places, or couriers bearing important secret messages, or sportsmen with guns on their shoulders. More humbly, they pretended to be peasants driving their cattle in front of them, or porters pushing their carts, or footmen dressed in the livery of a wealthy lord. Others travelled only at night on rarely frequented roads and spent the days hiding in barns, beneath the hay, or deep in thick forest.

Huguenots of the maritime provinces found freedom on French, English, and Dutch ships. The captains of these vessels hid them with the merchandise or in empty barrels where only the bunghole let them have air to breathe. Even persons previously living in the lap of luxury were ready to trust themselves in small open boats and crowded conditions. Charles Weiss reports that a noble of Normandy, the Count de Maranie

> crossed the English channel in a boat of seven tons in mid-winter, with forty persons, among whom were several pregnant women. Surprised by a storm, he remained long at sea, and with no hope of succor, tortured by hunger himself, the Countess and all the passengers, reduced for their sole nourishment to a little melted snow, with which they quenched their burning thirst, and moistened the lips of their weeping children, until half dead, they landed on the shores of England.[21]

Individuals living on the west coast of France counted on being transported in English, Dutch, or Huguenot-owned ships. Although coast-guards closely guarded the ports, their thrifty skippers were ready to run the risk of discovery for extraordinary gains from the escapees. They would wait until midnight, when the Huguenots could board their ships without discovery, especially if it were a sequestered part of the coast, and then carried them to the Channel Isles or to Plymouth. The other danger of seafaring was encountering of pirates. Two Protestants, for instance, wrote to ask for their deliverance from the Turks in Algiers. On June 6, 1687, they had boarded a boat with refugees coming from England and going to Holland, when three boats coming from Algiers captured them. One of the Algerian boats was then captured by a French warship. The letter mentions the presence of Huguenots working as slaves in Algiers—twenty-six women and girls, six or seven little children, and, among men, five ministers, three gentlemen and three postulants.[22]

Those who lived in or near Paris took the north as the direction of escape, as the Flemish border was only about one hundred miles away. According to Henry M. Baird,

> The method was to leave Paris about midnight on a market-day since the gates were opened more readily than on other days. Before dawn the travellers found themselves near to Senlis; the next stage of their journey could well be Saint-Quentin. Here in a home serving as a rendezvous, they remained until a suitably convenient time for their guides to convey them over the water. The guides made the Huguenots dress as peasants and each drove a donkey before them.[23]

The intrepidity and the resolution of the emigrating Huguenots become more evident when one considers the adventures of individual women. One of the hardest and longest was the journey to freedom undertaken by Judith Guiton Manigault. She left her home invaded by dragoons at night with the soldiers in their beds and, as she reports, "abandoning to them our house and all that it contained. Well knowing that we should be sought for in every direction, we remained ten days concealed at Romans in Dauphine, at the home of a good woman who had no thought of betraying us." Embarking at London on their way to America (where they arrived by making a long circuit through Holland and Germany), she records,

> . . . we suffered every kind of misfortune. The red fever broke out aboard the ship; and many of us died and among them our aged mother. We touched at the island of Bermuda, where the vessel that carried us was seized. We spent all our money there and it was with great difficulty that we procured a passage on board of another ship. New misfortune awaited us in Carolina. At the end of eighteen months, we lost our eldest brother, who succumbed to such unusual fatigue. So that, after our departure from France, he endured all that was possible to suffer. I was six months without tasting bread, working beside like a slave; and during three or four years, I never had the wherewithal completely to satisfy the hunger which devoured me. And yet, God accomplished great things in our favor by giving us the strength necessary to support these trials.

She concludes with a characteristic Huguenot tribute to God: "God gave us marvellous grace to have been able to resist all kinds of trial. I believe that if I wished to give you a detailed account of all our adventures, I would never have finished. It is enough that God had pity on me and changed my lot to one more happy, may glory be rendered to Him."[24]

Another account of the dangers of escape from France for Huguenot families concerns Mary Roussel, the granddaughter of a close friend of

Farel, the great early French reformer. Her father had died as a Protestant prisoner in his own house. Mary Roussel's mother, together with two boys, had reached Calais safely on their way to England. Mary's task was to follow with two other brothers aged eight and four. She dressed herself like a peasant girl and placed the two boys on panniers on a donkey's back, covering them with vegetable and fruit, charging the boys neither to speak nor move whatever might happen on the road. They travelled by night, but the latter part of the journey had to be completed during the day. Suddenly, a party of dragoons appeared, demanding to know what was in the baskets. Before she could reply, one of them drew his sword and plunged it into the pannier where the four year old boy was hiding. No cry was heard, nor was there any movement. The soldiers assumed all was well and galloped away. Immediately after they were out of sight, their sister removed the fruits and vegetables from the pannier, and, as the little boy lifted his arms to her, she saw that he was covered with blood from a severe cut on one arm. He had clearly understood that, if he cried, the lives of all three would be lost. Frank, the wounded lad, later had a daughter, Esther Benzeville, who wrote the account of Mary Roussel's flight in *Historical Tales for Young Protestants* for the Religious Tract Society, edited by Crosse.[25]

Another brave Huguenot lady was Marie de La Rochefoucauld, wife of the Chevalier de Champagne. That lady wrote, "On the 10th of April, 1687, my four daughters and two youngest boys . . . left La Rochelle. The head of a wine cask was knocked out; the wine emptied into the sea, and they were put inside the cask." The vessel in which they sailed was one of only eighteen tons and they paid twelve hundred francs for the passage. The escape was undertaken in two detachments, including Madame herself, her eldest son and a maidservant. They had to walk several leagues to a secluded beach, and a boat rowed them three leagues to the friendly vessel. The lady's report continues in her own words: "We were put down into the hold upon a quantity of salt, and for eight days we remained there well concealed, the ship being at anchor. The vessel was searched without our being discovered. We set sail and arrived at Falmouth eight days after, not without trepidation and great risk."[26]

An even more courageous heroine was Mademoiselle Guichard, who, in 1689, was governess of the family of the Marquis de Montvaillant. This castle, the home of the marquis, was used as a prison, and among the prisoners was a Huguenot theological student and preacher, Monsieur Roman. Hearing that he was to be executed the next morning, she planned his rescue, attempting it at midnight. It required her to be sure that the guards were asleep, then to find a way to open the prison door; disengage the prisoner's bonds and lead him to a room in the castle where there was a window looking toward the outer side of the walls. From there he could descend thence to a wall of great height and escape. No suspicion fell on her, but only on the marquis and owner of the castle who had once been a Protestant. He, therefore, became in danger of persecution. To save the marquis, she had the courage to confess. She was publicly whipped by the executioners and, for some years, was imprisoned at Sommiers. In 1696, she set out for England by way of Switzerland, Germany, and Holland.[27]

There is a very detailed account of the escape from France of Suzanne de Robillard at sixteen years of age. She later became the mother of the celebrated General de la Motte Fouque. She promised the captain of a small English ship the sum of two hundred *livres* a head for the five children accompanying her to England—half to be paid at the outset and half at the conclusion of the voyage in Exeter. At 8:00 p.m., she brought with her two boys, two girls arrived at 1:00 a.m., and she begged the captain to take another young sister whom she adored. At 2:00 a.m. that same night, four seamen carried her (with her sister in her arms), bearing them on their shoulders and hid them in a safe place on the boat. They were seven days at sea and the captain supplied biscuits, peas, and salted vegetables, but their sea-sickness prevented much consumption of food.

They finally reached Falmouth—approximately thirty leagues short of the promised Exeter. The captain asked for the other half of the money; she refused and complained to the mayor of Falmouth, who insisted that the captain take them to the location promised. The next day at 10:00 a. m., they reentered the ship which took them toward Tapson, a small port fairly near to Exeter. In this deserted spot, she visited a minister, who knew Latin, because the captain knew no French, but had some Latin, and she knew no English. The captain took two of the four *louis d'or* she retained to book a small boat to take them to Tapson itself, where they arrived the next day. At Exeter, in great joy, she met her mother and her brother.

Shortly theraftrer, they decided, because King James II of England was a Catholic, to choose a safer haven for Protestants. After six months in London, they moved to the neighborhood of La Haye, called Voorburg, where their father found them. He left for England as a captain of cavalry, and afterward, he went with Schomberg's troops to Ireland, fell ill, and died. Her story demonstrates the hazard of escape, the advantage of wealth, and the courage of a Huguenot youngster.[28]

There was also the escape from France of a distinguished minister of Charenton, the Rev. Peter Allix. Like all ministers, he was given only forty-eight hours to leave the country. After a narrow escape from the officer sent to arrest him, he arrived in Calais the evening of the day he sailed. The story is given in his own words:

> When I saw, in 1685, in the month of August, that we were certainly to be destroyed, I sent to England under another name my boxes of divinity that were seized by the King's commissary in my study, having then taken my resolution by the encouragement of my lord of Salisbury to take my sanctuary in England and hoping that I would prosecute my studies with some comfort. The Edict of Nantes being revoked the 21st of October the same year, I was commanded the same day to set out from Paris at a distance of two miles. I had no time granted but to get a pass from Msgr. de Menars, the intendant, who kept me very late by his fair proposals and promises. The same night, I went to Saint-Denis. When I went from Saint-Denis to Abbeville, I met there the Marquis de Ruvigny, the father, who came from England and offered me all the offices I could expect from his friendship and favor in England. As I knew he had more favors at court, I thanked him, and I would not make use of a letter that he made his son write to the Countess of Tyrconnel, who was there at Calais, with a yacht for England that I might have an easy passage in her yacht. I came to England and was very happy not to have any use of the recommendation of Mr. Ruvigny to the Countess because the order of stopping me came to Calais the same night on which I was gone in the morning, having made a narrow escape from death by the fury and brutish humours of the Mayor of Calais."[29]

The great concern to take their children into exile is a characteristic of almost every migration narrative. This makes it clear, as Henry A. Du Pont wrote, that "The fugitives [became] much more numerous after the issuance of the abominable edict in regard to the kidnapping of children."[30] He is referring to the Edict of June 17, 1681, that authorized the 'conversion' of any Huguenot child over seven years of age who would be placed in a Catholic institution with all expenses paid by the family.

In conclusion, it must be noted that many refugees did not settle in the first country they reached. The notable divine, Dr. Abbadie provides a good example. He first went to Berlin, where he ministered during the 1680's and then accompanied Marshal Schomberg to Holland, England, and Ireland. Upon returning to London, he became minister of the Savoy Church, and in 1699, dean of Killaloe in Ireland; he died at Marylebone, London, in 1727. He is an excellent example of the peregrinations of the Huguenot refugees.

A letter from the Rev. G. Baux provides insight into the refugees' awareness of the possibilities provided in other countries for both receiving alms and for finding employment. Baux writes to his brother in France who abjured his Protestant faith and he describes the general condition of the refugees: "those who work with their hands are the happiest as they have abandoned little and can work on the land in most places." The majority of the gentlefolk were, so he claims, widely dispersed in Brandenburg, England, Switzerland, or Holland. The early arrival of military officers from the French army was easily accommodated. About twenty outstanding officers received pensions, some of two hundred francs, and others according to their needs. Although the ministers received the best treatment, the army officers were second best.

Many ministers, he adds, were happier than they had been in France. About six hundred of them emigrated, and all in Holland found posts. Those in Switzerland, however, outnumbered the vacancies and had to "eat up their money". The most miserable, he reports, were doctors, advocates, procurers, and all public officers as well, as no one had done anything for them. They had, however, been able to live on the collections provided in England.

His lengthy letter concludes that the Swiss would give refugees money just to encourage them to leave. On the Rhine, several churches gave each person thirty sous, and much the same in Holland, while in Brandenburg, the misery was great. In England, the refugees were supported a little better. He adds,

> Many have transported themselves to Boston, Salem, New York, which are the countries in America dependent on the English King. Those who bring five or six hundred crowns with them are there established most happily for themselves and for their descendants, and I believe they made a good choice. That is why those from the coast of Royan, La Tremblade, Marennes, Ré, Oléron and La Rochelle make this choice.[31]

It would be a mistake to assume that the vast majority of the Huguenots were almost penniless in arriving in their foster country. In fact, money flew into Holland and England after the Revocation. According to King Louis XIV's ambassador in London, the London Mint had already melted 960 thousand *louis d'or* by 1687.[32] Along with the rich came thousands who were uncomfortably poor, and England and Holland gave them the support they needed in occupations and charitable grants. In the words of Peter Minet: "Few of the newcomers owned much capital and the fact that most of them were able not only to survive, but to thrive, was due to the discipline, industry, energy and endurance, which they had inherited from their forebears who had been obliged to acquire the art of survival on the continent."[33]

Whatever journey the Huguenots had to undertake, it was a journey of endurance, faith, hope, and charity; endurance through the days of darkness and the belief that life would triumph; faith that God would be with them as they escaped the Land of Egypt; hope that the land they reached would be the promised land; and charity which they both received and extended to one other.

Notes

1. Weiss in his *Histoire des Réfugiés Protestants de France*, (New York: Stringer and Townseed, 1854), 11 and Poole in his *Huguenots of the Dispersion*, (London: Macmillan, 1880), 168–169. According to George A. Rothrock, in his *The Huguenots: 1. A Biography of a Minority*, (Chicago: Nelson Hall, 1979), 178: "Most modern scholars think the numbers were a total of two hundred thousand, perhaps 1 percent of the population of Louis XIV's France"

2. See his *Huguenot Heritage. The History and Contributions of the Huguenots in Britain*. (London: Routledge and Keagan Paul, 1985), 24. Wills and Testaments, Deeds of Property, Records of Alms, and Records of the Galleys often furnish material as to the refugees' origins.

3. South Carolina Historical Society: Crottet Mss., piece n. 37.

4. S. Mours, "Essai d'évaluation de la population Protestante réformée au XVIIè et XVIIIè siècles.", *B.S.H.P.F.*, vol. 104 (1958), 1–24; see also his "Essai sommaire de géographie du Protestantisme réformé français au XVIIè. siècle" *B.S.H.P.F.* vol. 111(1965), 303–321 and *B.S.H.P.F*, 112 (1966), 19–36. See also, Bernard Cotteret, *The Huguenots in England*, (Cambridge: Cambridge U. P., 1991) who provides a map indicating that of the total French exiles in England 37 percent came from Poitou, 25 percent from Normandy, 7.8 percent from Saintonge, 7.3 percent from Picardy, 3 percent from the Ile de France, and 2.5 percent from Languedoc. These figures apply only to the late seventeenth century immigration.

5. Ch. Baird, *Huguenot Emigration to America*, 249.

6. *The Minutes of the Consistory of the French Church in London, Threadneedle St., 1679–1692*, Quarto series, (Huguenot Society of London. 1994).

7. W.H. Foote, *The Huguenots or Reformed French Church*, (Richmond, Va.: Presbyterian Committee of Publication, 1870), 76f.

8. The Churches, runnning out of funds, also encouraged such emigration see the entries for Feb.4, 1680, assisting families halted from going to Carolina because of contrary winds, Feb.15, 1685, when two elders will discuss with Sir Peter Colleton and William Penn the conditions they offer to refugees and Oct.13, 1689, when Threadneedle St. provides a pastor for the Boston Church. *The minutes of the Consistory of the French Church in London, Threadneedle St., 1679–1692*. Quarto series. (Huguenot Society of London: 1994). Respectively on 31, 143, and 312.

9. David C. A. Agnew, *Protestant Exiles from France*, (Edinburgh: Paterson, 1885), vol. 2, 250.

10. De Janzé, *Les Huguenots. Cent ans de persécution*, 291.

11. Robin Gwynn, *Huguenot Heritage*, 1–8.

12. Gwynn, *Huguenot Heritage*, 57 f.

13. Tessa Murdoch, ed., *The Quiet Conquest. The Huguenots, 1685–1985*, (London: Museum of London, 1985) Introduction.

14. Marc-André Bédard, "La présence Protestante en Nouvelle-France" *Canada's Huguenot heritage,* (Toronto: La Société Historique de Queébec, 1987), 165–66.

15. Georges Chinard, *Les Refugiés Huguenots en Amérique* (Paris: 1925), 14.

16. See Elie Benoît, *Histoire de l'Edit de Nantes*, 3 vols. (Delft: 1694/5; repub. London: Dunton) vol. 3, 973–975.

17. George Chinard,. *Les Refugiés Huguenots en Amérique* and Charles Baird, *History of the Huguenot Emigration to America.*

18. See R.D. Porcher's article on rice culture in South Carolina. In *Transactions of the Huguenot Society of South Carolina*, vol. 92, 1–24. About propaganda to attract the Huguenots to America see Rochefort, *Histoire naturalle et morale des iles Antilles de l'Amerique,* and the London pamphlet *Plantation work, the work of this generation* (1682), and the Dutch *Plan pour former un établissement en Caroline* (1686) as well as *Remarques sur la Nouvelle relation de la Caroline par un gentilhomme francais,* all quoted by G. Chinard, *Les Refugies Huguenots en Amérique* (Paris: 1925).

19. Elie Benoit,. *Histoire de l'Edit de Nantes,* (Delft & London: Dutton, 1694/5) vol. 3, part 2, 948 ff.

20. Charles Baird, *Huguenot Emigration to America*, vol.1, 7.

21. Charles Weiss, *History of the French Refugees* (New York: Stringer and Townsend, 1854) vol. 1, 110. The same story is recalled by W.H. Foote, *The Huguenots or Reformed French Church* (Richmond, Va.: Presbyterian Committee of Publication, 1870), 385.

22. F.R.J. Knetsen,. "Deux lettres de Protestants captifs à Alger de 1687" *B.S.H.P.F.*, vol.110, 54–56. See also, in the same volume, another letter by M. de la Mothe de Jourdan appealing on their behalf

23. Henry M. Baird, *Huguenots and the Revocation of the Edict of Nantes*, vol.2, 75.

24. George Bancroft, *History of the United States* (Boston: Little, 1839), vol.2, 180–181. This also appears in Charles Baird's *History of the Huguenot Emigration to America*, II, 396–97.

25. The story was summarized in David C.A. Agnew, *Protestant exiles from France . . . in Great Britain and Ireland*, vol.2, 350 f.

26. Agnew, *Protestant exiles*, vol.2, 142. For a fuller account see "The Journal of Mme. de Champagne" in *P.H.S.L.*, vol.13, 454–473.

27. Agnew, *Protestant exiles*, vol.2, 349-50.
28. *B.S.H.P.F.*, vol.17, 486-495 summarized.
29. *P.H.S.L.*, vol.13, no. 6, 625 ff. The fear he felt made his English awkward as well.
30. H. Dupont, *The Story of the Huguenots*, 14.
31. Letter of Reverend G. Baux in the *B.S.H.P.F.*, vol. 43 and 46 ff. The writer seems to have been misinformed about the situation of refugees in Brandenburg, where they received considerable sums of money and help to build villages and practice their trades.
32. De Janzé. *Les Huguenots*, 249.
33. Peter B. Minet, "A Huguenot Pilgrimage to Nîmes" *P.H.S.L.* vol.21, 238.

Chapter 4

Huguenot Faith and Character

It is strange that so many books on the contributions of the Huguenots make little or no attempt to analyze the faith that sustained them. They tend to concentrate on the historical, rather than the theological point of view. This chapter, therefore, attempts to analyze Huguenot faith and ethics as well as the discipline that maintained them.

Central to the convictions of the Huguenots was the Calvinist doctrine of predestination, with its assurance of the election of the faithful by God, regardless of human worthiness, and the character-sustaining conviction, which guarantees immortality after death in heaven. Only such a belief made it possible for Huguenots bound on their journey to the galleys in Marseilles or elsewhere to withstand the deadening darkness of the painful chain gangs, or, the vicious whippings on the boats for refusing to bow as the Catholic Mass went by. The same conviction fortified the heroic endurance of the faithful Protestant women who spent years in the prison of the Tour of Constance.

Cephas Carrière, for instance, wrote from the galleys to the pastor of a French Church at Erlanger:

> I consider myself happier in this location than in palaces where I would not be given the freedom to serve my God. We have often pondered about this between us and we bless him for having called us to suffer for the truth. Grant us always the help of your holy prayers, so that God gives us the strength to pursue the course of our lives with patience, so that, having done God's will, we might obtain the promise.[1]

The belief that suffering was essential to the mettle of a soul came directly from the founder of their doctrine. Calvin, indeed, wrote in a letter to the Duke of Somerset on October 22, 1548, "As doctrine is the soul of the Church for quickening, so discipline and correction are like the nerves to sustain the body in a state of health and vigor." He has also written in his magnum opus, *The Institutes of the Christian Religion,* Book III, ch. 21, the following definition:

> In conformity to the clear teaching of Scripture, we assert by an eternal and immutable counsel God hath once for all determined both whom He would admit to salvation and whom He would condemn to destruction. We affirm that this counsel, as far as it concerns the elect, is founded on his gratuitous mercy, totally irrespective of human merit: but that for those whom he devotes to condemnation, the gate of life is closed by a just and irreprehensible but incomprehensible judgment.

A.J. Grant comments on this citation:

> The Huguenots of France and the Puritans of the seventeenth century are not to be understood unless we remember always that they faced life with the temper that this doctrine gave them. They were the chosen soldiers of God in a war where victory was certain.[2]

It was discipline that characterized all levels of Calvinist Church government, at the local consistory where the elders, with the pastor, guarded the quality of Church membership, and at the higher levels of the Classis or Colloquy, which represented many churches in one area. The Colloquies sent representatives both clerical and lay to the Provincial Synods and they, in turn, to the National Synods, which ensured the uniformity of Protestant belief and behavior throughout France. Antoine Court, the virtual reviver of the French Protestant Church vividly expresses Calvinistic determination, which declared:

> How splendid it is to sacrifice oneself to God, even sacrificing the closest relationships as well as the dearest objects of our liberty, and even our life itself . . . Never lose that view of this perfect felicity, in the imitation of the Lord Jesus, the chief of our profession—because of the joy that like him you are offered to suffer the cross: scorn the ignominy, and like him you will be seated on the right of the throne of God.[3]

What were the motivations of the Huguenots? Clearly, they had a profound sense of direct individual responsibility to God in their consciences, combined with a deep trust in the Providence of God. The everyday conviction of the justice of Providence strengthened the character of a refugee pastor, Jacob de Rouffignac: he admitted that he feared long illnesses only and acknowledged that for the rest, because he had confidence in no human means, he depended solely on God's Providence.[4]

An even stronger conviction is reflected in the impressive songs of the *Plainte des Fidèles Persécutés* that mark their resignation to Divine Providence in 1686. They believed their torments were a result of the united forces of Satan so that:

> Mourir pour Dieu sont des délices;
>   Et quand dans ces grands sacrifices,
> Par une vive foi l'âme soutient le corps,
>   C'est les plus cruels supplices
> Que les héros chrétiens se montrent les plus forts.

The third stanza has these stirring lines:

>   Dieu se fera de pierres vives
> Une église au milieu des plus affreux déserts,
>   Et sur de plus heureuses rives
>   D'autres temples étant ouverts,
>   A nos familles fugitives
> Leurs langues et leurs voix aujourd'hui si captives
> Béniront hautement le Dieu de l'univers.[5]

The extraordinary strength of Huguenot faith is excellently expressed in the letters of Jean Mascarène, both written in 1687, two years after the Revocation of the Edict of Nantes. One, written to his wife on May 7, tells how he replied to a judge who urged him to recant for the sake of tranquillity. Mascarène reported:

> I replied, declaring as in the sight of God it was not out of obstinacy that I persevered in my religion, but because I recognized it to be true, pure and conformed to the word of God. I am ready, said I, to follow the Savior whithersoever He may call me. He gave up everything for me. He came to die for me upon a cross. I am constrained to abandon everything for Him and to suffer everything for the love of Him.[6]

In the second letter written by him to his lawyer, there is the same determined faith:

> For although my religion is regarded as a crime, and I see full well that but for my religion, I should not be in the state of which I am, I do not seek to justify myself of this pretended crime and I prefer to continue a criminal after this fashion rather than recover all that I have lost. [through the dragoons] All discussion apart, I am persuaded of the truth of my religion. My conscience has no relish for the religion that is offered me. I have an insuperable aversion to hypocrisy, and I am of the opinion that the only thing that can lead us to embrace a religion is the knowledge we have of God and what He has done for us, for love and gratitude that we ought to have towards Him, the knowledge and love of the truth, the fear of an infinite and everlasting misery, and the hope of a perfect and everlasting blessedness.[7]

Unquestionably, both courage and control were essential for the Huguenots. Edouard Privat properly insists that the person who aspired neither to heroism, nor to martyrdom, nor to asceticism would have found it difficult to live by these convictions. He adds that from 1650 to 1700, the Calvinists were hunted, massacred, ejected from their towns and expelled from their callings. It required enormous personal courage to endure the hostility and the repression, which not all Huguenots possessed. Even apart from persecution, Privat insists that the daily life of Protestants was difficult and austere. The religion of the Huguenots, in addition, was a constraining moral demand, which obliged him to control the most elementary inclinations, separating him from the places where the folk of villages and towns found diversions. It was hard to be unable to take part in balls, feasts, and pilgrimages, privileged moments in which the local community was welded, but Huguenots could not because they were forbidden to as Calvinists.[8]

Some Huguenots were clearly more courageous than others. Only one fifth emigrated. It would, however, be a mistake to think that the abnegation of Protestantism was judged lightly by either ministers or laity, which can be confirmed by the service of *reconnaissance*, that the Ecclesiastical Court of Guernsey required apostates to attend. Eighty-seven renegades thus repented between April 1686 and 1720.

Dame Marie-Anne du Vivier of Bayeux in Normandy, Adrien Viel of Caen, and Jean Pichon of Alençon, for instance received the consolation of the peace at the local church worship on the following Sunday. The service required the three persons to kneel at the foot of the pulpit of Saint Peter Port Church. Meanwhile, at this extraordinary assembly, they repeated, word for word after the pastor the following:

> We, Marie-Anne du Vivier, Adrien Viel and Jean Pichon, recognize here the presence of God and of this Holy Assembly; that we have grievously and extraordinarily sinned in having attended Mass; and by thus doing renouncing the Reformation: and the purity of the Gospel; by which we are most hurt: and sorry to have committed such a sin: to the great dishonor of the Almighty; and at the danger and peril of our souls and with the bad example we have given to the Faithful: this is why we here protest before God and before this assembly that we are whole-heartedly sorry and afflicted in our souls for having committed this horrible sin: we appeal most humbly to all-merciful God to forgive us this great and this enormous sin and all the others which we committed: promising solemnly never to offend Him again in this manner: And we pray you most urgently: all you who are present here: to help us continually by your prayers; for you to join specially with us in the humble and hearty prayer which we adress to Almighty God in saying: Our Father which art in Heaven etc. . . .[9]

This service of confession is touching in its solemnity and its full acknowledgment of sins against God and the people of God, affirming that the three humble sinners are "grieved with all our heart and afflicted in our souls"—all appropriately done while kneeling. Indeed, the Consistory of the French Church in London spent eight entire days to reintegrate in the Protestant confession those who had forsworn it in France. On the first Sunday of May 1686, it rehabilitated 114 fugitives and 497 in May 1687.[10]

Several persecuted Protestants were strikingly heroic. One of the most remarkable exponents of courage was that of the last Protestant minister hanged in France for his faith, namely François Rochette, who in 1762, sang on the scaffold a citation from Psalm 118:24 "This is the day the Lord has made; Let us rejoice and be glad in it."[11]

What are the prominent traits of the Huguenot character? Reverence, chastity, frugality, sobriety and industry characterize it—these are its leading qualities. Robert D. Gwynn has written that one is impressed by not only their combination of faith, resolution, and endurance, but also their potentially profitable connections, their need as refugees to apply themselves to whatever they undertook, and consequently, their exceptional degree of motivation, their preparedness to experiment and (if need be) to migrate anew and start again. Given good fortune, such qualities could be turned to profitable account . . . and this is precisely what happened.[12]

Their hard work was also aided by the fact that their counterparts, the Catholics, had many more religious holidays than the Protestants who were limited to Sundays, with the rare occasional provision of a weekday planned by a local church to provide a deeper religious commitment. Catholics were prohibited from work on 105 Saints' days, they worked for 260 days, while Protestant worked for 310 days in a year. This earned them the respect and sympathies of Colbert and the king.

Furthermore, Huguenots had to bear a financial burden for maintaining their religion. That was the support of the ministry that the faithful had to undertake. It was easier for the Catholics, apart from national support, because priests were single and Protestants usually were married. In addition, the pastor was obliged by ecclesiastical discipline to meet his copastors periodically at colloquies or synods, and these expenses were also the responsibility of the faithful laity.[13]

Huguenots also manifested other qualities. They had a capacity for mutual assistance and remarkable adaptability.[14] A striking example of this is found in an Irish Huguenot, William Lunel. He started as a draper in Dublin, but when his father died in 1720, he struggled during the next seven years with many difficulties, including extreme poverty. Finally, however, he succeeded in building up a flourishing wholesale trade with the Norwegian vessels that visited the port. To accomplish this, he had mastered the Norwegian language.[15] This application of hard work to improve a new opportunity seemed typical of Huguenots.

G.L. Lee also supplies other examples of Huguenot ingenuity and energy. She notes that James Rivet Vigiem who came to Ireland as a poor distressed Protestant in Cork in 1685, had become mayor of Galway by 1703, and David La Touche, who, at the Peace of Ryswick, was supported by only a small pension, became not only a wealthy manufacturer, but even the founder of the leading Dublin Bank.[16]

These qualities were not typical of the Huguenots of the seventeenth century only. Anglican Bishop Jewel, in the reign of Queen Elizabeth, had already thought highly of the Huguenots who had found their way to England. Of them, he said: "They labor truly, they live sparefully. They are good examples of virtue, travail, faith and patience. The towns in which they abide are happy, for God doth follow them with His blessings."[17] Jewel would have a special reason for appreciating these emigrants—he had been an emigrant himself during the reign of Queen Mary the Catholic.

Daniel Benoît is one of the few French commentators to write about the Huguenot character and its piety. If asked to give an example of the purest type of the Huguenot character, he replied unhesitatingly, "See here: Calvin."[18]

Benoît was most impressed by the Huguenot fear of the Eternal, which he characterized as the respectful fear of a child eager to obey his father, rather than the servile fear of the slave. He was also impressed by Huguenot veracity, by their endurance and readiness for all sacrifices for the faith. Surprisingly, these resplendent virtues were enhanced by a profound humility.

Daniel Benoît, however, also pointed out that these virtues sometimes exhibited the defects of their qualities. For example, their intense dislike of idolatry led them to pillage Catholic churches, and they were a little too eager to find divine intervention in ordinary affairs. They also tended to practice reverse discrimination by excluding Catholics from employment in the cities, such as Nîmes or Uzès, where they were a majority. Besides, the result of extreme persecution led them occasionally to express their feelings of resentment and their thirst for revenge.[19]

If, however, one compares French Huguenots with the contemporaneous Puritans of England, who were also Calvinists, there is one difference.

The French Calvinists manifested a greater cheerfulness of spirit and a love for the beautiful as seen in their artistry and their cultivation of flowers, while their love of liberty led them to be more pliant on secondary issues because of their passion for tolerance.[20]

An impressive tribute to Huguenot character was offered by E.W. Montague, when proposing a motion in the English House of Commons for the naturalization of French Protestants in England. He pointed out that the king of Prussia invited and supported Huguenots for them to fertilize what had been before an almost barren Prussia. This was, he claimed, the result of the Calvinistic ethic that assigned great value to work, regarding it as the practical exercises of a calling appointed by God and, therefore, both as Divine worship and a means of averting temptation. He added that the distinctive feature of Calvin's creed was the belief in Election by Grace. This dictated an absolute duty to consider oneself chosen and to combat all doubts as temptations. The individual responsibility common to large groups of refugees produced the Huguenot traits of reverence, chastity, sobriety, frugality, industry, and honesty.[21]

What were the sources of Huguenot faith and spirituality? Primarily, it was the Bible as the record of God's Revelation upon which all the other components were based. These included Divine worship not only on Sundays, but also involved family and personal devotions practiced at home. Sunday services contained prayers led by the minister, including an important confession of sins that ended with a plea for God's forgiveness, expressions of gratitude to God, with petitions for the sick, the suffering, and the needy. The climax of worship was the sermon in which a portion of the Bible was expounded both doctrinally and ethically. The congregation's part in worship was limited to the recital of the Apostles' Creed and, significantly, the singing of the metrical Psalms translated and versified by Bèza (Calvin's successor in Geneva) and the poet Marot. Of great importance were the celebrations of the Sacrament of Holy Communion, including the sermon and Holy Baptism. Communion was celebrated approximately every three months and carefully guarded by forbidding the unworthy to attend until they were pardoned.

Baptism was for both children and adults. The former required parents solemnly to promise to rear their children in the Christian faith. The latter insisted on promises of solemn personal commitment to God. Finally, the ordination of the clergy demanded a thoroughness of training, which was dispensed in the famous academies of France, in Geneva, and in Lausanne.

At the outset, it is essential to recognize that the theology underlying Huguenot spirituality and worship is Calvinist. The very source of the liturgy used on Sundays was based on early worship in Frankfurt and, subsequently, in Geneva, planned by John Calvin. Its vigorous relevance was twofold: First, it was not in Latin as that of Roman Catholicism but in the living vernacular—the French language—and, secondly, it was dominated by proclaiming the essential obedience of faith as responsibility to God. Also, the poor were remembered generously in annual collections and boxes were placed in Protestant shops to receive the free-will offerings of those charitably disposed.[22] The Consistory, it should be mentioned, was especially solicitous of impoverished artisans, providing not only food and clothing but also even the tools required for their craft.[23]

Perhaps the most distinctive feature of Huguenot worship was the singing of the metrical psalms. The vivid psalms of Théodore de Bèze and of Clément Marot had caught the imagination of the Huguenots, and they were sung at every service. When they first appeared, they were so appealing that Catholics as well as Protestants sang them to popular tunes. In fact, they became almost secular in their use by members of the French court and were sung by soldiers at campfires, whistled by ploughmen and carters, and even sung by ladies and their lovers. It is to Calvin's credit that he moved the metrical Psalms from their secular milieu into the worship of the French Reformed Church at Strasbourg. Many were sung to the solemn joyful melodies of Bourgeois.[24] This use of metrical psalmody was defended by asking, "What is more suitable for God's praise than God's own Word?" Furthermore, metrical psalms expressed praise, strengthened faith in difficult times and provided marching orders for God's soldiers. This was the lyrical element essential to worship as rejoicing.

Reciting St. Paul's account of the Last Supper in the First Epistle to the Corinthians, chapter II, verses 23–26, emphasized the fidelity of the Protestant Church to Christ's foundation of Holy Communion. It stressed vividly that this was the night of Christ's betrayal, that Christ is the food of the soul, and that the bread and the wine symbolize his body and blood.

Public services were open to the public, but not the Lord's Supper, which was restricted to members in good standing. Persons of dubious reputation were excluded. For example, the censure of the Consistory in La Rochelle in the 1570s reached even those whom civil law could not touch: "the greedy, the drunken, the blasphemers, the unchaste were one after another brought to account for their irregularities. In this way it came about that a well-known merchant of the city, having speculated in wheat during a season of scarcity in the means of subsistence, was condemned "to make public reparation, and give the poor the profit he had realized."[25] The Consistory prepared a list of persons considered worthy to receive Holy Communion and to these were distributed *méreaux* or small leaden tokens. These were required for all that presented themselves on the four great occasions at which the Lord's Supper was celebrated—at Christmas, Easter, Pentecost, and the first Sunday of September.[26]

Interestingly enough, although prayers and preaching were part of the celebrations of Baptism and Marriage, they could not be used at the burial of the dead. This was to prevent the idea that superstitious concepts of the efficacy of supplications on their behalf should seem to be countenanced.[27]

It is extremely difficult to imagine the context of Protestant worship in France and to visualize the interior of their churches, because Louis XIV destroyed every one of them by 1685, and there survived only a few engraved depictions of major churches such as those of Charenton, Rouen, and Lyon. Otherwise, there are only verbal descriptions of their interiors.

The largest of their temples was that of Charenton in the vicinity of Paris, and that of Rouen was not much smaller. Charenton's temple, which emulated the palace of Solomon, could accommodate four thousand persons. Designed by the royal architect, Salomon de Brosse, himself a Huguenot, it was a rectangle with two galleries and an imposing central pulpit. The elders of the congregation occupied the important seats close to the pulpit. Its stone exterior was exposed to the light by six round-topped long windows in the front, and four shorter ones below that were were divided by a large portal. Each long side of the building had eight long round-topped windows, a portal, and seven short round-topped windows below.[28] This structure of 1624 was demolished by the order of Louis XIV on October 22, 1685. On its roof was an impressive bell-tower, which bore a *Fleur de Lys* in token of its loyalty to the king of France.

Another renowned temple was that at the village of Quévilly, built to serve the citizens of Rouen. They could reach it only by crossing the Seine and traveling several weary miles to attend the services. The Rouen temple was an old, but substantial, building made of wood, also capped by a lantern and the *Fleur de Lys*. Its ground plan was a twelve-sided figure, almost one hundred feet in diameter and seventy feet high. Sixty windows kept it well lit. It could comfortably contain over four thousand worshippers, similar to that of Charenton.[29] The temple of La Rochelle was built to the plans of Philibert Delorme and was octagonal in shape.

The style of Huguenot temples was deliberately evangelical, emphasizing the absolute primacy of the Gospel proclaimed in the preaching. The temple at Lyon was built on a circular plan, with three entrances at ground level, and a gallery running round the inside. It was reached by a double staircase on the exterior and was lit by four oval windows. The pulpit occupied a central position and the congregation sat on a series of plain wooden benches. The men were seated apart from the women and wore their hats according to custom.[30]

What of the more typical and smaller temples of France? They refused to use the Roman Catholic traditional cross-shaped plan. So they were usually rectangular or oval in shape, and well-lit, according to that mixture of baroque and classical style, which was typical of French architecture. Each enabled the minister's voice to be easily heard from the central pulpit. Above the pulpit was a notice board, displaying the Ten Commandments of the Law. Other alternatives were to display the Lord's Prayer or the Apostles' Creed. There were neither stained glasswindows nor statues; neither crosses nor impressive altars. Usually, at the front, a raised platform on one side faced the pulpit on the other side. The raised platform was used by the Consistory, other Church officials, or visiting government officials.

The communion plates preserved in countries to which the Huguenots escaped, such as England and Ireland, speak eloquently of the high honor with which the Lord's Supper was held. E.A. Jones provides some impressive examples in his *The Old Silver Sacramental Vessels of Foreign Protestant Churches in England* (1908). He includes the silver chalice and the silver platter, both mounted on triple-ringed bases used by the Savoy Huguenot Church of London, dating from 1717 and used until 1737. The same book illustrates the chalice and paten of the French Church of Hoxton, the gift of Stephen Romilly. His third son became a prosperous jeweler and the father of an eminent lawyer, Sir Samuel Romilly. This communion plate, also of 1717, is slightly simpler in its silver pattern. Clearly, these shining objects to include the wine and the bread of the Lord's Supper indicate how much their donors honored the Sacrament.

Before one can appreciate the elevated standing of Protestant ministers in France, it is necessary to have some knowledge of the qualities of the leading ministers, as well as an awareness of the distinguished institutions in which they were trained.

Among the leading ministers at the time of the Revocation of the Edict of Nantes were Claude, who had been at Charenton from 1666 to 1685, and the writer of the famous treatise *The Complaints of the Protestants Cruelly Persecuted in the Kingdom of France*, which included the following passage:

> We protest against all the consequences of this Revocation; against the extinction of the exercise of our religion in the whole kingdom of France; against the infamies and the cruelties practiced upon our corpses, in refusing them burial, in casting them in unconsecrated places, whither they were disgracefully dragged on hurdles; against the abstraction of our children for the purpose of instructing them in the popish religion. We protest, above all, against that impious and detestable practice to which France still holds fast of making religion depend on the will of a mortal and corruptible prince, and of treating perseverance in faith as an act of rebellion and a state offence, which is in fact, to make of man a God.[31]

Other ministers from Charenton included Allix—a colleague of Claude—whom Louis XIV considered the finest speaker he had ever heard and who ministered at London's Savoy Church.[32] Mesnard, formerly at Charenton, became court preacher to William III in Holland and a canon of Windsor. Pierre Jurieu, another distinguished clergyman, defended the Reformed faith against Bossuet's damaging charges of changes in doctrine, and was renowned for his *Critical History of Dogmas*.

Among those who became famous preachers in Holland, was also Pierre Du Bosc, who became minister at Rotterdam, and was a keen exponent of the doctrines of St. Augustine, and Jacques Saurin, who became both a renowned and immensely popular minister at La Hague.

Other notable ministers included, Abbadie, the friend of Marshal Schomberg, who accompanied him first to Brandenburg, and later to England. Abbadie produced a notable exposition of the Divinity of Christ that even Roman Catholics admired. There was also the intrepid Pierre Daille, the virtual founder of the French Reformed Church of America, ministering in New Amsterdam, Boston, and New Paltz, who had been a professor of divinity at the Saumur Academy.

Some ministers foresaw the final defeat of seventeenth century Protestantism. Pierre Jurieu had said in 1682:

> If things continue at the present speed as in the last few years and particularly in the last few months, it won't be long before someone persuades the king that three quarters of the Huguenots of his kingdom have converted: he will be told that what's left is of no importance and deserves no consideration; thus he will be brought to suppress all the Edicts.[33]

This is exactly what happened.

Not all the ministers accepted the two most frequent alternative answers to the Revocation of the Edict of Nantes—either escape or abjuration. James Fontaine, for instance, rejected the attitude of patience and long-suffering prescribed by the Gospel. He advocated rebellion against the king: "My blood boiled under the sense of injury, and I desired earnestly that the Protestants should take up arms in a body, and offer resistance instead of waiting quietly to be slain like beasts at the shambles."[34]

There were several important training centers for the ministry, known as academies, in seventeenth century France, and each had its own distinctive emphasis. In common they prepared their students for preaching, for expounding the catechism, and for controversy, but they also provided general training. Several ministers belonged to pastoral dynasties, such as Claude, Daille, Basnage, Dumoulin, Chamier, Drelincourt, and Jurieu. Many important French pastors were trained in Geneva, especially in the earlier days, but in later years the majority were trained in France. This lasted until the middle and late eighteenth century when the Swiss center of Lausanne assumed the responsibility of preparing many of the preachers under Antoine Court for the "Church of the Désert."

The list of Protestant academies in France included Saumur, Sedan, Montpellier, Montauban, Puylaurens, Nîmes, Orange, Orthez, and Dié. These academies provided both secondary and postsecondary education in law and, occasionally, medicine. The eldest, at Nîmes, was founded as a municipal college, elevated to a college preparatory school, and later became a university, where a chair of theology was added in 1559. In 1598, the academy at Saumur was created, as well as that of Montauban. Both were proposed by a national Synod to which Henry IV had given the same privileges as other universities, such as that of conferring the degree of Bachelor and Master of Arts.

Other academies were Montpellier, which became attached to Nîmes in 1617; Orthez, founded in 1566 but closed in 1620; Orange, started in 1573; Sedan, an outstanding institution (founded in 1602 by the Duke of Bouillon), which had a wide curriculum, with courses in the classics, as well as in theology and law. The smallest academy was that of Dié, founded in 1604 for the Dauphiné.[35]

Although the Academies were founded primarily to train French Protestant ministers, they also trained young men in the area of general knowledge in the Faculty of Arts, for their betterment in civil society. The indispensable disciplines provided included philosophy and ancient languages such as Hebrew, Greek, and Latin. Theological studies for postulants lasted three years and regularly required entrants to have the M.A. degree. Teaching in theology comprised instruction in Christian doctrine and Christian ethics, careful Biblical exposition of the Old and New Testaments for sermons, linguistic preparation in Hebrew and Greek, and a capacity to cope with religious controversy, especially with the Roman Catholics.

The most distinguished academies included Saumur. Saumur's specialty was systematic theology. Its star professor was Moyse Amyrault, who had been taught by a Scottish Professor Cameron, a savant of Greek and Roman Classics. He wrote a six-volume history of ethics in which he interpreted the doctrine of predestination more gently than the severer formulation of the Synod of Dordrecht. Amyrault taught the renowned preachers Jean Métrezat, Michel le Faucheur, and Pierre Du Bosc. Jean Claude was also a pupil at Saumur. Basnage, a distinguished historian, was partly a product of Saumur where Louis Cappel, a founder of the discipline of modern historical criticism of the Bible, taught there for thirty-one years.

The centers containing academies also disseminated culture from their libraries, bookshops, and printing presses. Sedan City boasted two printers and Saumur a dozen bookshops. Moreover, their links with the major European theological controversies were great, especially of those on Predestination or Arminianism, which were closely parallel to those of Molinists and Jansenists in Catholicism. Sedan was more orthodox and Saumur more liberal giving some place to human cooperation with God. Its internationalism must have been stimulating: faculty and students came from Switzerland (Zurich, Neufchatel and Geneva), from Holland and from Scotland. Foreign professors, according to Solange Deyon, numbered as many as forty and some great savants were also included among them.[36]

Each academy almost had its own concentration and its own emphasis. Montauban concentrated on producing good students of Hebrew, while Saumur's stress was on systematic theology and church history. Sedan was noted for its orthodox Calvinism, while Nîmes concentrated on underlining the central importance of preaching, by having a daily sermon on week days and four on Sunday; it also stressed the importance of catechetical instruction.

Most Protestant sermons of the seventeenth century were strictly careful Scriptural expositions of exceptional fidelity, but there were few references to ancient theologians and even fewer citations from profane authors. There were, of course, great variations among the great preachers, but not of subject matter. They varied in emphasis and personality, including wit, a gift for and fondness for lively illustrations, logical analysis, and so forth. Some were good psychologists like Amyrault, others were good moralists, like Du Moulin, and Claude was a very popular exponent of Christian convictions and their ethical results.[37] With such effective training centers and such renowned preachers to imitate, the level of preaching in small towns and villages must have been above average in the quality of religious convictions and its effectiveness in character building.

The quality of the piety that sustained Huguenot character is finely expressed in the following prayer of Jean Claude:

> O Lord Jesus, Savior all powerful, who seem to have abandoned your heritage to the violence of your enemies, return to us in your clemency, with the same compassion which brought you to the cross for our salvation. You know the weaknesses and feebleness of those who serve you, so do not allow them, O Great God, to be exposed to temptations greater than those you have given them. You see that Satan marches ahead more and more to scatter those that you have bought back with your blood; limit his violence and his fury. Grant, O divine Savior, that your children may resist him and their courage make him leave them . . . May your mercy which made the disciple which denied you a fully distinguished Apostle revive those who have fallen by feebleness and timidity. Strengthen those who still stand upright. You see the scattered sheep. Be in yourself the Shepherd, You who make those find You who are not even looking for You, and make in your pity those who seek You with zeal and ardor. You who say to the sinner, "I have forgiven the penalty of your sin", immediately he says,"I have sinned", make your people test again your mercy and your love in your gift, giving marks of repentance. Grant, O all powerful God, that they may confess you courageously before men, to the end that hoping genuinely that you will recognize them again, that they may hear your promise to your faithful: "Come, blessed of my father, possess as your heritage the kingdom prepared for you from the foundation of the world." God grant that we may find ourselves among the number of the blessed. Amen.[38]

A gentleman named Beverley Tucker of Williamsburg, in a letter of 1846, wrote that he had found one general character running through the race of Huguenots: "They are sprightly and full of fire, but serious and earnest in all essentials, seeming something like a cross between the Frenchman and the Scotchman." Referring to the ancestors of residents of New Paltz in New York State, another reporter wrote: "To serve God according to the dictates of their conscience was with them paramount to everything else. They were a race of men who exemplified to perfection the Christian Soldier . . . These men brought their Bibles and Psalm books with them. While they abandoned the places of their fathers' sepulchers, they clung to the Gospel." Yet a third writer adds: "There are none that I have any knowledge of who have inherited the principles and spirit of their ancestors to an equal degree with this people . . . You might suppose that they are abrupt, plain, blunt and vulgar, but such is not the case. They have still enough of French politeness and suavity of manners, mixed with Dutch sincerity and hospitality and the French spirit still survives sufficiently in the fondness for gaiety in dress and equipage, to keep up with the fashions of the day."[39]

In conclusion, we shall leave the final evaluation of Huguenot character and faith, to Robin Gwynn, that outstanding historian:

> The refugees who left France were devoted to the Huguenot cause. Usually determined and principled men and women, they believed that to serve God gave meaning to life. This belief engendered a strong sense of accountability for their actions, and both in turn fostered the virtues which have marked out the Huguenots and so many of their descendants: frugality, hard work, upright behavior, responsibility, sobriety. The key to understanding them, their willingness to abandon their homeland, their frequent eventual prosperity in the places to which they went, the time they were prepared to devote to their churches, is one and the same: their concept of, and commitment to serve a God infinitely greater than themselves.[40]

Notes

1. Gaston Tournier, *Les galères de France et les galériens Protestants des XVIIè et XVIIIè siècles*, (Mas Soubeyran: Musée du Désert, 1943), appendices and 281.
2. A J. Grant, *The Huguenots*, (London: Oxford University Press: 1934), 18.
3. Our translation of a letter sent to M. Espinès. See *B.S.H.P.F*, vol 29, 409 f.
4. *P.H.S.L.*, vol.5, 255.
5. *Plaintes des Fidèles Persécutés*, in *B.S.H.P.F.*, vol. 5, 312–15.
6. Cited in Charles Baird's *Huguenot Emigration to America*, (New York: Dodd, Mead & Co., 1885.), vol.2, 365.
7. Charles Baird, *Huguenot Emigration to America*, vol.2, 347.
8. Ed. Privat, *Histoire des Protestants de France* (Toulouse: 1977), 33.
9. F.D.G. de Schickler, *Les Eglises du Refuge en Angleterre*, (Paris: Fischbacher, 1892), vol.2, 524–25. Nous Marie-Anne du Vivier, Adrien Viel, et Jean Pichon, reconnaissons icy la présence de Dieu et de cette Sainte Assemblée; que nous avons péché grièvement et d'une façon extraordinaire d'avoir été à la Messe; et par ce moyen renonçant à la Réformation: et à la pureté de l'Evangile; ce dont nous sommes très sensiblement touchez: et marris d'avoir comis un tell péché: au grand déshonneur du Dieu Tout-Puissant; et au danger et périll de nos âmes: et au mauvais exemple que nous avons donné aux Fidèles: C'est pourquoi nous protestons ici devant Dieu; et devant cette Assemblée que nous sommes marris de tout notre coeur: et affligez en nos âmes: d'avoir comis cet horrible péché: Nous supplions très-humblement le Dieu de toutes miséricordes; de nous pardonner ce grand et cet énorme péché; et tous les autres que nous avons comis: promettant sollenellement de ne l'offenser jamais de telle sorte: Et nous vous prions très-instamment: vous tous qui êtes icy présens: de nous assister continuellement de vos prières; de vous joindre particulièrement avec nous dans l'humble et cordiale prière que nous adressons au Dieu Tout-puissant, en disant: Notre Père qui es aux Cieux etc.
10. De Janzé, *Les Huguenots: Cent Ans de Persécution*, (Paris: Grasset, 1886), 232.
11. Tessa Murdoch, compiler, *The Quiet Conquest. The Huguenots, 1685–1985*, (London: The London Museum, 1985), introduction.
12. Robert Gwynn, *The Huguenot Heritage: the History and the Contributions of the Huguenots in Britain*, (London: Routledge and Kegan Paul, 1985), 175.
13. Privat, *Histoire des Protestants*, 34.

Huguenot Faith and Character 73

14. See John Lawson, *A Journal of a thousand miles traveled through several Nations of the Indians*, (London: 1701). Quoted by Donald Douglas, *The Huguenot*, (New York: Dutton, 1954), 374, he wrote: "There are about seventy families seated on this river, who live as decently and happily as any planter in these southward parts of America. The French being a temperate, industrious people, some of them bringing very little of effects, yet by their endeavor and mutual assistance among themselves, have outstripped our English, who brought with them large fortunes, though, as it seems, less endeavor to manage their talent to the best advantage."

15. Reported by G.L. Lee in *The Huguenot Settlements in Ireland*, (London: Longmans, 1936), 244.

16. *Ibid.*

17. R. W. Gelf, ed. *The Works of Bishop Jewel*, vol.7, 265.

18. D. Benoît, *Du Caractére Huguenot et de la Transformation de la Piété Protestante*, (Paris: Fischbacher: 1892), 4.

19. D. Benoît, *Du Caractère Huguenot . . .*, 12–18.

20. See Charles Baird, *Huguenot Emigration to America*, vol.2, 253 for a testimonial on the Huguenots of Massachussetts.

21. Tessa Murdoch, ed. *The Quiet Conquest. The Huguenots, 1685–1985*, introduction, 13.

22. The emphasis on independence of judgment and social interdependence was part of the reason that Bonrepaus, born François Dusson, converted to Catholicism. Protestantism meant a certain belief in republicanism, which he could not tolerate. See Laurent Dingli, "Bonrepaus et la Révocation de l'Edit de Nantes," *B.S.H.P.F.*, 141.

23. Henry Baird, *The Huguenots and the Revocation of the Edict of Nantes*, (New York: C. Scribners,1895) vol.1, 373.

24. Calvin wrote in his preface to the Geneva edition of Marot's *Fifty Psalms* in 1545: "Nous ne trouvons meilleures chansons ni plus propres pour se faire que les Psaumes de David, lesquis le Saint Esprit lui a dictez et faits."

25. Louis Delmas, *The Huguenots of La Rochelle*, (New York: Anson D.F., Randolph and Co., 1880), 55.

26. Henry Baird, *The Huguenots*, vol.1, 381.

27. Henry Baird, *The Huguenots*, vol.1, 382.

28. Henry Baird, *The Huguenots*, vol.1, 377. Also see W.H. Foote, *The Huguenots, or French Reformed Church*. Richmond: Presbyterian Committee of Publication, 1870), 371.

29. *Histoire de la persécution faite à l'Eglise de Rouen sur la fin du dernier siècle*, (Rotterdam: 1704. Repr. Rouen: L. Deshays, 1874), 2.

30. Tessa Murdoch, ed., *The Quiet Conquest*, 26, facing which there are two etchings of Charenton and of Lyon.

31. The edition of Cologne, 1743, 89.

32. Charles Weiss, *The History of the French Protestant Refugees from the Revocation of the Edict of Nantes to Our Days*. (New York: Stringer and Townsend, 1854), vol.2, 79.

33. Pierre Jurieu, *Derniers efforts de l'innocence affligée*. 2 vols. (The Hague: 1682), vol.1, 30.

34. See Fontaine, *Memoirs of a Huguenot family*, (London: 1885; repr. 1986), 92. In the Fontaine family two sisters recanted whilst one remained firm in her faith.

35. S. Mours, *Les Eglises Réformées en France*, (Paris and Strasbourg: 1958), 15.

36. Solange Deyon, "Les Académies protestantes en France" in *B.S.H.P.F.*, vol 135, (1984), 77–85.

37. Edouard Privat, ed., *Histoire des Protestants*, 132–33.

38. Jean Claude, *Recueil de Sermons sur divers Textes de l'Ecriture Sainte par Jean Claude Ministre dans l'Eglise Réformée de Paris*, (Genève: Samuel de Tourne, 1690), II0.

39. These citations are derived from *Transactions of the Huguenot Society of North Carolina*, vol.4, 53–60, in turn deriving from the pages of *The Christian Intelligencer*, 1845.

40. Robin Gwynn, *Huguenot Heritage*, (London: Routledge and Keagan Paul, 1985), 109. The call for simplicity appears in this will from Arnaud Bruneau Chabocière: "I ask those who will give me the last rites to have me buried and put underground according to the manner of the Reformed Churches in France, with the least ceremony and the simplest manner possible" *Wills and Testaments*. Charlestown, County of South Carolina. November 1694.

Chapter 5

Ministers and Doctors; Military Men and Politicians

The faith of Huguenot refugees led to the mention of a few distinguished names. Yet, merely to record that they included Field Marshal Ligonier, Romilly, the political reformer, the author Defoe, and Garrick the actor, denies the combined contributions that they were able to make. Indeed, snapshots of grouped prominent Huguenots, according to their callings, enable us to assess better their brilliant contribution to the English-speaking world.

Twentieth century popular culture has led us to consider the army and the Church as antithetical. In the sixteenth and seventeenth century, however, they were considered as two forms of public service, available to the nobleman's eldest and second sons. Neither the commanders nor the higher churchmen were salaried. Higher Churchmen and Officers came from the same noble stock, ideally—a family with a sense of public service and tradition, whom the king rewarded with a generous pension.[1] Both were highly respected vocations, sometimes combined in such ecclesiastical orders as the Order of Malta. The third son might become a merchant or a lawyer, professions that were respected in the seventeenth century, when ecclesiastical vocations dropped dramatically.

The noble sons of Protestants followed the tradition but also turned to the professions of medicine and law, as did the Protestant middle-class. Because they included men who were accustomed to thinking for themselves, it is hardly surprising that these professions formed the largest groups of French Protestant exiles.

Huguenot Ministers

As propagators of the unwanted faith, divines were the first to be targeted. For the greater part, they had either to conform or to emigrate because their churches were destroyed. They were expelled as a group from France at the Revocation, because they expounded the Protestantism repulsive to Louis XIV's vision of national unity.

To deify the Protestant clergy, because they became the victims of oppression, would be a mistake. Perhaps the most surprising information about the Protestant clergy is that a fairly high proportion had abjured their faith. Nineteenth century historians, who admired and defended the Huguenots, may well have exaggerated their fidelity. More recent writers assert that the quality of the ministry was not as high as previously judged. For example, Daniel Ligou, in his historical evaluation of the Protestant clergy of seventeenth century France, claims that the general quality of those ministers was low. He also claims that out of the approximately seven hundred pastors, serving a similar number of churches, no fewer than seventy-four were deposed by the Synods—half for immorality and half for heresy—and that thirty of them apostatized. He concludes that, at the moment of the Revocation, a quarter or perhaps a third rejoined the dominant Church and very few returned from the refuge to support the fidelity of loyal reformed congregations.[2]

Furthermore, Emile G. Léonard in his *Histoire générale du Protestantisme* concluded that a third of the pastors had abjured.[3] That may be surprising, but considering the alternatives of uncertain emigration, hanging, or the galleys, one cannot be shocked. It is difficult, however, to accept the all too easy exoneration of a writer who abnegated abnegation thus: "Nonetheless, one rediscovers that throughout France, the habitual sentiment was that apostasy is only pronounced by the lips, and the heart remains as it was formerly."[4] But abnegation, by either ministers or the laity, usually left wounds that were not easily healed.

According to Gwynn, the best modern historian of the contribution of the Huguenot refugees in England, ministers were the most eminent refugee group.[5] In English-speaking lands, the number of divines was high. The reason was the warm welcome given them by the Church of England, if they would only conform liturgically to Anglicanism and be reordained. This conditional welcome, however, seemed an implied insult to French Reformed ministers, as former Catholic priests were accepted by the Church of England without reordination.

When the French divines reached England, therefore, their first problem was to decide whether to seek acceptance in the ministry of the Presbyterian Churches (which were considered nonconformist like the Independents—later known as Congregationalists—or the Baptists), or to accept Anglican appointments. Despite the need for reordination already mentioned, the major attraction of Anglicanization was that it offered far more affluence than nonconformity and that it had more pastoral vacancies.

Huguenot ministers objected, however, to the fact that Anglican worship was more formal and its ceremonial more impressive than its French equivalent. If they became Anglican ministers, they would have to wear surplices and use a liturgy with required responses.

The counter arguments were twofold. After being regarded as a despised minority in France, it was appealing to belong to the majority, and also to be allowed to conduct worship in their native tongue, even if they had to wear a surplice. In addition, their sons would be welcomed to Oxford and Cambridge Universities, which were closed to the sons of ministers affiliated with the Presbyterian or other English nonconformist Churches.

There was also another advantage in that there already existed a completely satisfactory French translation of the Book of Common Prayer—the work of a native of the Channel Isles, one Jean Durel. In 1662, he had received the appointment of a chaplain-in-ordinary to King Charles II as well as a reward of prebends successively at Salisbury, Windsor, and Durham, which he held contemporaneously.

Although they were legally responsible to the Bishop of London, the clergy who accepted Anglican reordination were delighted that their new church was firmly antipapal, and they were at last in a land where they could be both Protestant and profess the religion of the king. It was apparently the laity who were more averse to ritualism, and many of them joined the French non-Anglican churches in London and in the larger provincial towns.[6]

It is interesting to note that, even in conformist French churches, they were not, like Anglicans, required to kneel when receiving communion. In fact, the churches under flexible Anglican supervision allowed ministers to maintain some of their traditions in worship. When conducting worship, they were permitted to wear their black gowns rather than white Anglican surplices, were not required to make the sign of the cross, and could still encourage Psalm-singing, which had been such a distinctive and popular ritual in France.

In London, in 1700, congregations in the West End, supported the Savoy Church, while in the East End, the many weavers felt happier worshipping in one of the nonconformist congregations located in Spitalfields, including Saint Jean l'Hopital, La Patente, Artillery (two), Crispin Street, Pearl Street, Wheeler Street, and Du Marché.

All this according to Robin Gwynn proves that "for most Huguenots, the Anglican liturgy was second-best." He estimates that during the 1680s, under pressure, there were perhaps two refugees worshipping as conformists to every three nonconformists, but that by the death of William III in 1702, following a decade of freedom of choice, there were three times as many nonconformists as conformists.[7]

Some distinguished divines, such as Jean Claude, the famous minister of the leading Protestant Church at Charenton outside Paris, were greatly displeased by the popularity of turning Anglican on the part of French parsons. They regarded it as a betrayal of the Reformed tradition, but a considerable number of ministers accepted the Anglican blandishments. John Dryden ridiculed the conformists in his poem, "The Hind and the Panther", published in 1687.

> Think you your new French proselytes are come
> To starve abroad, because they starv'd at home?
> Your benefices twinkl'd from afar.
> They found the new Messiah by the star:
> Those Swisses fight on any side for pay,
> And 'tis the living that conforms, not they.
> Mark with what management their bribes divide
> Some stick to you and some to t'other side,
> That many churches may for many mouths provide
> More vacant pulpits wou'd, more converts make
> All wou'd have latitude enough to take;
> The rest unbenefic'd, your sects maintain;
> For ordinations without cure are vain,
> And chamber practice is a silent gain.

Although Claude did not settle in England as his son was a minister in Holland, his criticism was widely read by emigrés there and in England.

Jacques Abbadie had also preached at Charenton. Initially, he was invited by the Elector Frederic William to be minister to the Church in Berlin in 1680. While there, he wrote La vérité de la religion chrétienne. In 1688, Marshal Schomberg begged Abbadie to accompany him to England following the Prince of Orange and his army. He was nominated pastor of the Savoy Church in London, but he did not acclimatize well. Then, King William III recommended him to the deanery of St Patrick's in Dublin, but he had to decline because of his ignorance of English. In exchange, he accepted the deanery of Killaloe in Ireland, the duties of which gave him ample time to write. His "Treatise of the Truth of the Christian Religion", was admired even by outstanding Catholics such as Madame de Sévigné, who commented, "It is the most divine of all books."

His other publications included sermons, letters on the real presence of Christ in the Eucharist, a treatise on the divinity of Christ, a defense of the British nation, panegyrics on Mary, the wife of William III, and on Queen Anne, on the truth of the Christian Reformed religion, and the triumph of Providence and of religion.

Pierre Allix had been educated at the top Protestant academies at Saumur and Sedan. Three years after reaching London, he wrote, "A Defense of the Christian Religion" in 1688. In 1690, he was made canon and treasurer of Salisbury cathedral and was awarded the doctorate of Divinity from both Oxford and Cambridge Universities. He published thirty-one books.[8] His son, also named Pierre, who gained his D.D. in Cambridge, was named dean of Gloucester in 1729 and a year later, dean of Ely cathedral.

Given the education they had received in the academies, one need not wonder at how many of the refugee divines were also men of letters, now included in *The Dictionary of National Biography*. Such were James Abbadie, Luke de Beaulieu, Charles Daubuz, Pierre Drelincourt, David Durand, Isaac Dubourdieu, Jean Armand Dubourdieu, John Jortin, Claude Grostête de la Mothe, Michael Mallard, and Abraham Le Moine.

René Bertheau and Samuel de l'Angle both received an honorary Oxford D.D. Motteux of Rouen translated *Don Quixote* and the works of Rabelais into English. Pierre Jurieu, the indefatigable writer of sixty books, spent a short stay in England. His book, *Traité de la dévotion*, of 1678, went into its twenty-eighth edition and was translated into English. He also wrote an important treatise to counter the exposition of the Catholic religion by Bishop Bossuet: *Le Préservatif contre le changement de Religion*. Two other notable divines were Philip Duval, D.D., F.R.S., canon of Windsor and Balthasar Regis, chaplain to Wake, the Archbishop of Canterbury, later chaplain to George I and George II and also a canon of Windsor.[9]

The life of the convert Jean Gagnier was also fascinating. Born in a Catholic family, he began his career as a regular canon of St Geneviève, but became disabused of the catholic religion and fled to London in 1685. The bishop of Worcester made him his chaplain, and took him to Oxford, where he taught Hebrew for several years. Finally, in 1715, Gagnier was appointed professor of Oriental languages at Oxford, where he wrote several books. These included *L'Eglise Romaine convaincue de dépravation, d'idolatrie et d'anti-christianisme en forme de lettre* (The Hague, 1706) and several volumes using his expertise in Hebraic Studies as well as a life of Mohammed.[10]

James Cappel, professor of Hebrew at Saumur when only nineteen, came to London and ministered at the French Church at Threadneedle Street for many years. For part of that time, he was professor of Oriental languages at the Dissenters' College in London known as Hoxton Square Academy.

Another outstanding divine came from the legal profession. Rev. Claude Grostête de la Mothe, a doctor of civil law from the University of Orléans, practiced law in Paris and changed to divinity in 1675. He then became minister of the town of Lisy and was clerk of the last Protestant Provincial Council held at Lisy in 1683. His books treated the following themes— the inspiration of the New Testament, Dialogues on the fraternal correspondance of the Church of England with Foreign Churches, appeals for the galley slaves in France, and critiques of three Camisard prophets. He also commemorated the general active sympathy for the French Protestants in Britain in a book entitled, *Caritas Anglicana*. Before his death, he had a long and serious illness and, characteristically, wrote several sermons on Christian duties during convalescence.[11]

From England, divines sometimes passed to Ireland, as did Abbadie, or to America, like Pierre Daillé. A distinguished divine in Ireland was Dean Drelincourt, the sixth son of Charles Drelincourt of Charenton, the latter being renowned as "Cher trésor de Calvin." He was appointed chaplain to the duke of Ormond, and, after graduating from the University of Dublin, precentor of the Cathedral in Dublin. In 1691, he became dean of Armagh.[12]

The Huguenot divine who traveled farthest from France was Pierre Daillé, formerly professor of divinity at Saumur Academy, who first fled to London and then to North America. He is the real founder of the French Reformed Church in America. He arrived first in New York and worked there for thirteen years, founding the French churches in Hackensack, Staten Island, and New Paltz. He then went to Boston where he remained from 1682 to 1685.[13]

Often families produced several ministers, who tended to be dispersed in various countries. Two brother ministers, the Meynards, were initially separated but finally reunited. The elder, John Meynard, was a minister at Charenton. At first a refugee in Holland, he was, like Abbadie, brought to England by the Prince of Orange, future King William III of England, who appointed him canon of Windsor. His younger brother, Philippe Meynard, found refuge in Denmark, where he remained for five years. Queen Charlotte Amelia made him her chaplain and minister of the French Church in Copenhagen. He then accepted the invitation to become minister of the French Chapel Royal of St. James in London.

As previously mentioned, many distinguished divines had also settled in Holland, including Claude, Basnage, Martin, Benoit, and Saurin. The most eminent banished ministers were appointed to academies established in Rotterdam, Leiden, and Utrecht.[14] That was also true of the Prioleaus—Elizea Prioleau, grandfather of Elie Prioleau, minister of the French Church in Charleston, was minister in Jonjac near Pons.[15]

If lawyers became divines, sometimes so did physicians. Elie Bouhéreau obtained his M.D. at the University of Orange, because all other universities in France were forbidden to graduate Protestant medical students. He became pastor of one of the French congregations in Dublin and received Anglican ordination. He also became Librarian of the Marsh Library in Dublin. He published two books, one on the appropriate way to select a doctor, and the second entitled *The Treatise of Origen against Celsus*.

Often in the seventeenth century a clergyman's son became himself a clergyman. Both in England and Ireland many descendants of Huguenot refugees became distinguished divines. In England, the descendants of the brilliant Master-Surgeon, Gaston Martineau are renowned as Anglican or Unitarian clergy. Arthur Martineau, former fellow of Trinity College, Cambridge, was appointed chaplain to the archbishop of Canterbury and later became prebendary of St. Paul's Cathedral in London. The Rev. James Martineau, a superb liturgist in the Unitarian Church, held pastorates in Liverpool for twenty-four years and in London for thirteen years.[16] Most of this time he combined these duties with serving as a professor at the leading Unitarian Theological College in Manchester, which later moved to London. He wrote four important books, each providing a rational analysis of its theme. These were *The Rationale of Religious Enquiry, The Types of Ethical Theory, A Study of Religion*, and *The Seat of Authority in Religion*.

In the nineteenth century, the most influential leaders of the Anglican Church were also descendants of French Huguenot refugees. Cardinal John Henry Newman was descended on his mother's side from the Foudriniers, and professor Edward Bouverie Pusey, who headed the Tractarian movement when his friend Newman left the Church of England for the Roman Catholic Church, was, as his second name implies, descended from the Bouveries. In fact, he was the grandson of Jacob Bouverie, the first Viscount Folkestone. That two descendants of the Huguenots led the Tractarian or Romanizing movement in England shocked other descendants of Huguenots. Agnew reports how angry Dr. Merle D'Aubigné was in his critique of Pusey: "There was formed, even among Anglican ministers—sacerdotal habits—superstitious doctrines of Rome— which vividly attack the Reformation . . . The Reformation" said this

Anglican priest "was not a Pentecost. I look on it as a Flood, an act of divine vengeance."[17] He would have rejoiced that another descendant of Huguenots, the Rev. William Romaine, was one of the leaders of the Evangelical movement in the Church of England during the latter half of the eighteenth century. Another important evangelical of Huguenot descent was the Rev. Joseph Sortain, an eminent minister of the Countess of Huntingdon's Connexion. Of him Agnew writes: "His ministry at Brighton was one of great fidelity, brillance and celebrity . . ." The Victorian novelist W. M. Thackeray wrote that he was "The most accomplished orator I have ever heard in my life."[18]

In Ireland the Tranche, or Trench family, also attained ecclesiastical distinction. One of them was the Most Rev. P. le Poer Trench who was bishop of Waterford, then of Elfin, and, finally, archbishop of Tuam in 1819. Another, the Most Rev. Richard Chenevix Trench became archbishop of Dublin and a much-admired writer. Dr. Henry William Magendie became successively canon of Windsor, canon of St Paul's cathedral, London, Bishop of Chester, and, finally, Bishop of Bangor.[19]

In Scotland, the Rev. Charles Hughes Terrot, also of Huguenot stock, became Bishop of the Scottish Episcopal Church in Edinburgh. He was a modest man who objected to being addressed as "My Lord", remarking that the Church makes Bishops, but the Crown makes Lords.

What, then, was the chief contribution of the Huguenot divines in England? In a word, it was teaching their congregations obedience to God as soldiers to their celestial general. It was instructing their congregations in the primary importance of conforming to the will of God as revealed in Holy Scripture both in public and in private. They exhorted their flocks to serve God by exhibiting the remarkable virtues of full accountability for all of their actions and the hard work, frugality, responsibility, and uprightness expected of Huguenots.

Huguenot Doctors

Many trained Protestant doctors had fled from France to England, because of religious affiliation during a period of two hundred years. Jean Bauhin, born at Amiens in 1511, and a surgeon to Queen Marguerite of Navarre, had removed from Paris to London where he remained from 1532 to 1535. From the late sixteenth century, several notable doctors are recorded in England, such as Gidéon de Laune (1565–1659), who was both minister and physician. His daughter married Peter Chamberlen. His two eldest sons practiced medicine with distinction. Gidéon served as apothecary to James I and was the first Master of the Society of Apothecaries.

Around the year 1572, at the time of the Massacre on St Bartholomew's Eve, Pierre Chamberlen, the second member of an outstanding medical family, fled from Paris to London where he practiced medicine in Mark Lane until 1613. The family is renowned for having invented the obstetric forceps and was notorious for keeping this a secret for three or four generations of the seventeenth century.

The first to seek refuge into England was Guillaume Chamberlen, who was admitted to communion in Southampton in 1569. His grandson, Hugh, published *The Accomplisht Guide to Midwifery*. The third to be christened Pierre was Queen Henrietta Maria's physician whom King Charles II recognized after the Restoration as having "attended our happy birth and being therefore one of our first servants."

Sir Théodore Turquet de Mayerne (1573–1655), who helped to form the Society of the Apothecaries, was not a refugee. Physician to Henry IV, he came to England at the invitation of King James I, received the honorary doctorate at Oxford and was knighted in 1624. Dr. Jean Colladon, who married Mayerne's niece came to England from Geneva, took his M.D. at Cambridge, became physician in ordinary to Charles II, and was knighted in 1664. Théodore Colladon, his son, also a physician, attended King William III. A protégé of Mayerne, Antoine Choqueux, was appointed sergeant-in-ordinary to the household of Charles I.

At the time of the Revocation, doctors had already been forbidden to practice their art for several years. Most of them, therefore, were not surprised by the rigidity of the ban. Some happy exceptions included a doctor from Vigan in the Cévennes, Charles Portales, Sr., who was thrown into prison, but seems to have been subsequently released, whereupon he continued in his profession.[20] W.R. Le Fanu claims that the complete list of medical emigrants to England numbered over 400, described as "docteurs-en-médecine," "chirurgiens," "apothicaires" or in similar terms for medical training or practice.

Other notable early refugee doctors in England were Jacques Primerose whose grandfather had been a surgeon in Scotland to King James VI and had followed him as surgeon to the throne of England, and James Fontaine who was appointed Surgeon-General of Ireland in 1661. Two other renowned doctors were Nicolas Le Fèvre and Denis Papin. Le Fèvre, who attended the freethinker Saint-Evremont for forty years, was appointed an apothecary to the household of Charles II in 1661. Denis Papin, born in Blois, graduated M.D. at Angers in 1669. He practiced in Paris, was assistant to the Dutch scientist Constantin Huygens at the Académie in Paris and came to London to help Robert Boyle the famous chemist. He will be discussed further as an eminent inventor. Another notable physician was Charles Drelincourt (son of the Dean of Armagh), doctor to both William of Orange and his wife.

Also worthy of note was a surgeon of Bergerac by the name of Gaston Martineau who fled France in 1685, settled in Norwich, and was the first of five generations of medical men. The most widely known was his grandson, Dr. Philip Meadows Martineau. The family produced the most famous Unitarian Divine, James Martineau.

Some doctors were accomplished in other fields. Among them, Matthieu Maty, a friend of Saint-Evremont, practiced in London from 1741 and became one of the early Librarians of the British Museum. Other friends of Saint-Evremont included Pierre Sylvester who also seems to have combined the medical and the divine profession by becoming a pastor at Parson's Drove and François de Mouginot who married the second daughter of the Marquis of Cagny.[21]

Claudius Amyand arrived as a refugee in 1688, having served as a surgeon in the Duke of Marlborough's army at victorious Blenheim; he became Sergeant-Surgeon to George II and master of the Company of Barber-Surgeons in 1731. His eldest son became Under-Secretary of State in 1750, and his second son was created Baronet. Paul Bussière, another surgeon and a famous anatomist, became a Fellow of the Royal Society in 1713 and a consultant at the final illness of Queen Caroline in 1737.[22]

It should be noted in passing that, between 1680 and 1720, sixteen Huguenots were elected Fellows of the Royal Society. Among the medical fellows, Paul Buissière and Pierre Silvestre contributed to the improvement of surgery through the private courses they offered on anatomy in England and the Dutch Republic. These improved the standards current in surgery as well as the confidence in which the medical men were held professionally. Another Fellow of the Royal Society was Abraham de Moivre, an excellent mathematician, supported by Sir Isaac Newton, to whom he had dedicated his Doctrine of Chances, a study of probability. Jean Théophilus Désaguliers was an itinerating public lecturer and brilliant scientist and inventor.

Other Huguenot Fellows of the Royal Society were David Durand, Peter de Maizeaux, Jean Chardin, and Peter Mark Roget of Thesaurus fame, a physician, who was its long-term Secretary. He invented the slide-rule.

Both ministers and doctors, therefore, were most likely to be librarians and men of letters. They included Henri Justel, son of a protestant minister, formerly the private secretary of Louis XIV, who fled just in time. An enthusiastic Protestant, he was close enough to the king to foresee exactly what was coming, received a letter of invitation to London in 1681, and sold his library to become warden of the Royal Library in St. James. Other librarians of note included Elie Bouhéreau, a physician, who became head of Archbishop Marsh's Public Library in Dublin and a Precentor at St. Patrick's Cathedral, and Paul Colomies, appointed Librarian at the Archbishop of Canterbury's Lambeth Palace.

Michel le Vassor, a convert from Catholicism wrote from London a history of the reign of Louis XIII in eleven years and was pensioned by William III. Abel Boyer, who had left for Holland with his uncle, a preacher, wrote educational books for learning French and an English-French dictionary.[23] Some became Professors at Oxford University, the historian Louis du Moulin and the orientalist, John Gagnier, for instance. Saint-Evremond studied in London, in the brilliant society of Hortense Mancini and wrote pamphlets such as "The conversation of the Marshall of Hocquincourt with Father Canaye", slyly satirizing what he considered the irrational fideism of the Roman Catholic Church.

Naturally prominent Huguenots would be interested in reason and education. In America, Thomas Hopkins Gallaudet became the founder of the first American institution for the deaf and dumb and Bawdoin, named after the Governor of Massachusetts, was celebrated in the foundation of Bowdoin College.

Outstanding Military Huguenots

There is much irony concerning the fate of military Huguenots, which makes the popular saying of cutting one's nose to spite one's face applicable to the policy of Louis XIV. Indeed, some of the strongest defenders of France became, because of circumstances, some of its fiercest slaughterers. Arthur Giraud Browning ends an important article with the following claim:

> I have now said enough to prove that the modern art of war owes more to the strategy, tactics, armament, organization and practical lessons of the Huguenots than to any other class of men, and it was exceedingly fortunate for England that their services were available when, at the close of the seventeenth and the beginning of the eighteenth centuries, she began to change her insular position for one of continental and imperial importance.[24]

The aristocratic military leaders of France were cordially welcomed in other countries, and the majority of them were Huguenots. These included the Prince of Tarentum, who served in the Dutch army; the Duke de la Trimeville in Hesse; the Count de Roye in Denmark; Count Beauveau who left for Brandenburg; and the Elector made Count de la Cave Major General and Privy Counselor, and Du Plessis Gauret was appointed commandant of Magdeburg and Spendau. The Marquis de Varennes became lieutenant-colonel in active service in Brandenberg, and his officers consisted chiefly of Huguenots.[25] The country to which the majority of the military went was Holland, where Prince William of Orange welcomed them with generous allowances of eighteen hundred livres for colonels, thirteen hundred for lieutenant-colonels, eleven hundred for majors, nine hundred for captains, five hundred for lieutenants, and four hundred livres for ensigns and cadets.[26] The Huguenots were a dominating element in the army William led from Naerden in Holland, which landed on the English coastal town of Torbay on November 15, 1688, to establish his right, through his wife, to the throne of England.

Leading officers in the Prince of Orange's army were outstanding because of the extraordinary skill military leaders had reached in earlier years in the well-trained armies of Louis XIII and XIV. Among them was the Count de Gassion, to whose advice Condé owed his victory at Rocroi; he was raised after the battle to the rank of marshal at the request of the young prince. Others, no less distinguished, were Marshal Guébriant, the conqueror of Alsace; Marshal the Duke de La Force who defeated the Spaniards at Carignan; the Duke of Lorraine, victorious in Italy and Germany; and the Duke of Rohan and Marshal of Chatillon who led Richelieu's armies to victory on the Northern frontiers of France. The most famous Huguenot general of all was Turenne, a supreme tactician, and Admiral Du Quesne, the conqueror of De Ruyter.[27]

Turenne's tactical method included a plan of moving in diagonal fashion against the flank of the enemy instead of moving against the front, as well as a plan to use detaining forces while retaining a central reserve. All this tactical mastery was familiar to de Schomberg and his colonels.

Frederick Duke of Schomberg was a marshal in France. Louis XIV initially tried to convert him, but, failing to convince him, asked him to stay, despite his refusal. He remained William III's leading tactician until the Battle of Le Boyne in Ireland, where he died. When Schomberg was struck down, he was encouraging Caillemotte's foot regiment, after its commander was mortally wounded, by pointing to the dragoons and papists on the Southern side of the river and shouting: "There are your persecutors! Forward, men, forward!"

Henri de Massue de Ruvigny had a similar experience. He served under Turenne and, because of his English connections—his sister had married Thomas Wriothesley—he was sent to conduct secret negotiations with Charles II. Having refused Louis XIV's offer, after the Revocation, to keep his present post as general, he fled to Holland and entered the service of William III. After distinguishing himself in Ireland, he was made Earl of Galway and was Lord Justice in Ireland. He even commanded the English forces allied to the Duke of Savoy in order to rescue the Vaudois and, in 1704, he commanded allied forces in Portugal during the War of the Spanish Succession. He died in 1720.

Other leading Huguenots in this army were Goulon, the chief of artillery, Cambon, the chief of engineers and three aides-de-camp: de L'Etang, La Mélonière, and the Marquis d'Arsellières. In addition, there were fifty-four Huguenot officers in the Blue and Red Guards and thirty-four in the Life Guards. William's expedition of fifteen thousand men included three entire regiments of French Infantry soldiers numbering twenty-two hundred and fifty men with seven hundred and thirty-six French officers. About eighty officers, trained under Condé and Turenne, were entrusted with the highest responsibilities in the expedition.[28]

To show the quality of Louis XIV's army, one should also mention some of the less exalted Huguenot officers who attained distinction in later years. Captain René de La Fausille, for instance, in La Caillemotte's regiment received six wounds at the battle of The Boyne; his son John became a major general in 1761. Brigadier Louis Petit helped to win the island of Minorca for the British army. Brig. Mark Anthony Moncal achieved this rank in the British Army by 1711, after distinguishing himself at Gibraltar in 1705. Brig. Samson de Lalo, colonel of the 28th foot regiment in 1701, and colonel of the Royal Scots Fusiliers in 1706, was promoted to brigadier in 1709; he died in action a few months later. Antoine du Perrier also fell at Malplaquet, and two of his great grandsons were knights, sheriffs, and mayors of Cork. Other notable soldiers were Majors Isaac Cuissy, Mollien, Henry Foubert, Abel Pellissier and Colonel La Fabrèque. La Fabrèque, a lieutenant in Schomberg's Horse Cavalry at the rank of captain in 1689, became a colonel of Carpenters' dragoons in 1707 at the battle of Almanza. Another colonel named Rieutort served in Ireland under William III and assisted in the relief of Gibraltar. He later became a chamberlain to the Elector Palatinate in Germany, but died at his Chelsea home in 1726. Thus, the careers of most of the officers who fought in King William's army proved to be impressive, judging by their later promotions and responsibilities.

As the years passed by, some men of Huguenot descent obtained military appointments of great distinction in England. This was particularly true in the Ligonier family. François Auguste Ligonier came to England in

1710 and was made a colonel of the thirteenth light dragoons. Jean-Louis Ligonier had come to England in 1697, and his bravery in the British Army in Flanders caught the attention of the commander, the Duke of Marlborough. In 1735, he was promoted to major-general and was ennobled as Viscount Ligonier of Enniskillen. Another member of the same family was Edward, Earl Ligonier, born in 1740, who became major-general in 1775.[29]

The same was true of naval officers. There were dynasties of Protestant mariners, some of them linked to famous Dutch mariners—Jean Gabaret, for instance. So much so that a letter from Seignelay on April 14, 1680 asking Navy administrators to deprive Huguenots gradually of jobs in the navy caused embarrassment. They initially retrieved clerical jobs from them, well aware that if they barred Huguenot officers from their posts, the French Navy would collapse. Louis XIV sent Bossuet to try to persuade Du Quesne to recant, but never forced him to do so. Yet, soon after his death, all sorts of pressures were applied to his wife and she finally gave in.[30]

In conclusion, many distinguished military leaders of Huguenot heritage came to Great Britain either directly or because they had joined the army of William the Stadtholder, who became king of England. Other high-ranking soldiers or sailors of Huguenot descent include Earl Ligonier of Ripley, a field marshal in the English Army and a cavalry expert, and Admiral Gambier of the British Navy.

In America, the leading generals of Huguenot stock were Sherman and Pershing, and the naval commanders included Decatur, Dewey, and Schley.

We have seen that the most distinguished sailor in France was Admiral Du Quesne. He was too old at the time of the Revocation to emigrate and was allowed to finish his days in peace. He died in 1688. It is intriguing to learn that in 1686, more than 800 sailors entered the navy of the United Provinces. Naval officers of Huguenot descent in England include Vice Admiral James Gambier who died in 1789. His nephew, bearing the same name became a full admiral, leading the bombardment of Copenhagen in 1807. Also in the napoleonic wars, both Sir John Laforey and his son, Sir Francis Laforey, became full admirals.[31]

These examples of success make it abundantly clear that in both the army and the navy, France lost much by the Revocation of the Edict of Nantes. The integrity, determination, perseverance, total reliability, and courage of the Huguenot character brought its own rewards to both soldiers and sailors in war and in peace.

Notable Huguenot Politicians

The perfect leader of the seventeenth century was a balance of War and Peace as embodied in the salons of Mars and Apollo in Versailles and the encomiastic literature pertaining to Louis XIV. The politician was the leader of peace, which is not surprising, given the distribution of professions in a noble family between elder son going to war and second son joining ecclesiastical orders, that some of the most influential politicians were not only lawyers, as we would expect nowadays, but also ecclesiastics. One must wait, however, until the middle of the eighteenth century to find politicians of real distinction and fame.

The most distinguished and honorable Huguenot politician in England, Ireland, and North America, was Samuel Romilly, the grandson of emigrants. Born of Huguenot stock from Montpellier in 1757, he became a lawyer trained at Gray's Inn and entered the House of Commons as solicitor-general in Grenville's ministry in 1806; he was knighted and chosen as a Privy Counselor that same year. He soon became almost as renowned as Wilberforce whose general aims he shared. His Parliamentary career focused on remedying injustice and cruelty. Within a week of taking office, he attended the Privy Council to examine a harsh naval lieutenant who caused three seamen, without any court-martial, to be flogged so severely that they died. The very next day, he sat beside Wilberforce in the House of Commons and readily gave him a promise to speak warmly in favor of a bill for establishing schools in every parish in England for the education of the poor, and in later sessions, he supported bills for the prevention of cruelty to animals. He was renowned as a reformer *sans peur et sans reproche*.[32]

In Ireland, the most notable politicians were the La Touche family. Lecky's *History of Ireland in the Eighteenth Century* records that, "In the last Irish Parliament, no less than five members of the name of La Touche, sat together in the House of Commons."[33]

It is, however, in North America that we find the largest and most notable list of persons of Huguenot ancestry who filled the very highest political offices. Alexander Hamilton, for instance, was born of a Huguenot mother, Rachael Faucette, in the island of Nevis in the Antilles. He became secretary of the treasury in Washington's cabinet. The most distinguished perhaps was Jean (John) Jay, born in New York in 1745, the eighth child of a citizen of La Rochelle, who escaped via England to South Carolina and then to New York State. After graduating from King's

College (later named Columbia University) as a lawyer, he was elected a representative of the first Congress at Philadelphia in 1774. Later, he became Chief Justice of New York and was elected President of the Congress in 1794, and in 1795, he was appointed Chief Justice of the United States. This is all together a striking series of responsibilities for one man to have assumed.[34] Two others, in addition to Jay, were three of the five presidents of the Continental Congress—Henry Laurens and Elias Boudinot.

Henry A. Dupont has written that the many descendants of the Huguenots include "four Presidents of the United States, Tyler, Grant, Garfield, and Roosevelt, whose descent in the female line is traced to the Huguenot families of Comtesse, De La Noix (Delano), Ballou, and De Vaux . . ."[35]

Notes

1. See also Abraham D Lavender, *French Huguenots*, (New York: P. Lang, 1990), 43. He remarks that in France, unlike in England, nobility and gentry did not form a common class and trade was forbidden to nobility.

2. Daniel Ligou, *Le Protestantisme en France de 1598 à 1715*, (Paris: Société d'édition d'Enseignement: 1968), 168.

3. Léonard, *Histoire générale du Protestantisme*, vol.2 , 346 and 375.

4. B.S.H.P.F, vol.40, 465. The French original concludes: "L'apostasie n'est prononcée que des lèvres; et que le coeur reste ce qu'il était jadis." For the regular abjuration formula for the bishopric of Chalons in 1685, see Annex III of Patrice Jacquelot de Chantemerle de Vilette, *Les Jacquelots Protestants du XVIè au XVIIIè siècle en Champagne et dans les pays étrangers*, (Paris: Chez l'auteur, 1994).

5. R. Gwynn, *Huguenot Heritage. The history and contributions of the Huguenots in Britain*, (London: Routledge and Keagan Paul, 1985), 85.

6. The issue of higher education of sons of pastors is mentioned by Elizabeth Labrousse in Irène Scouloudi, ed. *Huguenots in Britain and their French background*, (London: Macmillan: 1987), 151. On the primary issue see Bernard Cotteret, *Huguenots in England*, (Cambridge University Press, 1991), 173.

7. *Huguenot Heritage*, 103.

8. Eugene and Emile Haag, *La France protestante*, (Paris: Fischbacher, 1877), vol.1, columns 10–16, 146 and 153.

9. R. Gwynn, *Huguenot Heritage*, (London: Routledge and Kegan Paul: 1985), 86. Others who had Huguenot ancestors also contributed to religion. Vincent Perronet was actively associated with Charles and John Wesley and Anthony Bèzenet became a Quaker who emigrated to North America and was a staunch champion of the rights of African-Americans and Indians.

10. Emile Haag, *La France protestante*, vol.1, columns 784–85.

11. David C.A. Agnew, *Protestant Exiles*, vol.2, 241 ff.

12. David C.A. Agnew, *Protestant Exiles*, vol.2, 22.

13. Otto Zoff, *The Huguenots: Fighters for God and human freedom*, (New York: L.B. Fischer, 1942), 330.

14. Samuel Smiles, *The Huguenots: Their Settlements, Churches and Industries in England and Ireland*, (New York: Harper Bros, 1867), 178.

15. See Crottet Mss Collection. South Carolina Historical Society.

16. For an assessment of Martineau's liturgical gift, see Horton Davies, *Worship and Theology in England*, (London and Princeton: Oxford University Press, 1962), vol.4, 267-275.

17. Agnew, *Protestant Exiles*, vol.1, 224-25. "*Il s'est formé, même parmi des ministres anglicans—des habits sacerdotaux—des doctrines superstitieuses de Rome—et qui attaquent vivement la Réforme . . . La Réformation,*" said this Anglican priest, "*n'a pas été une Pentecôte. Je la regarde comme un déluge— un acte de vengeance divine.*"

18. Agnew, *Protestant Exiles* . . . II, 227.

19. Agnew, *Protestant Exiles*, vol.2, 228.

20. Prefatory note to *Mémoires inédits d'Abraham et d'Elie Marion sur la guerre des Cévennes*, (Paris: Fischbacher, 1931). Published also by the Huguenot Society of London, vol.34.

21. Briggs. "Some Huguenot friends of Saint Evremont" *P.H.S.L.*, (1977-82), 7-18.

22. W.R.Le Fanu, "Huguenot Refugee Doctors in England," *P.H.S.L.*, vol. 19, (1952-1958), 113-127.

23. Briggs. "Some Huguenot friends of Saint Evremont" *P.H.S.L.*, (1977-82), 7-18.

24. Browning. "The influence exerted by Huguenot Refugees of the Seventeenth and Early Eighteenth centuries upon the social and professional life of England", *P.H.S.L*, vol.17, 304-323.

25. William Henry Foote, *The Huguenots or French Reformed Church*, (Richmond, Va : Presbyterian Committee of Publication: 1870), 410-411.

26. Charles Weiss, *A History of the French Protestant Refugees from the Revocation of the Edict of Nantes to our own days*, (New York: Stringer and Townsend: 1859), vol.2, 22.

27. A.G. Browning, "The Influence of Huguenot Refugees." *P.H.S.L.*, vol.7, 304 ff.

28. Samuel Smiles, *The Huguenots*, 192.

29. D.C.A. Agnew, *Protestant Exiles*, vol.2, 325 f and 309f.

30. See Michel Verge-Franceschi, *Abraham Du Quesne. Huguenot et Marin du Roi-Soleil*, (Paris: France-Empire, 1992), 292 ff.

31. Samuel Smiles, *The Huguenots: Their Settlements, Churches and Industries in England and Ireland*, (New York: Harper Bros., 1867), 190.

32. Sir William J Collins, "Some notes on Sir Samuel Romilly and Etienne Dumont". *P.H.S.L.*, vol.12, no. 6, 461-485.

33. Lecky. *History of Ireland*, 302.

34. Eugène and Emile Haag, *La France Protestante*, (Paris: Fischbacher, 1877), vol.6, 59.

35. Henry A Dupont, *The Story of the Huguenots*, (Cambridge: Riverside Press: 1920), 33.

Chapter 6

The Contributions of Huguenot Manufacturers

In 1708, when Edward Montague proposed in the House of Commons a motion for the naturalization of French Protestants, he emphasized the advantages that their coming would bring to England. Citing the example of the ruler of Germany, who invited them in order to fertilize what previously had been an almost barren Prussia, he also stressed their capacity for hard work, their religious faith, and their admirable character. But even he could not have imagined the variety and the quality of the manufactures and, therefore, the savings that they would effect in the English economy. England would no longer be an importer of French manufactured goods, but even occasionally become itself an exporter. This chapter will concentrate on inventors' and manufacturers' achievements in England, Ireland, and America and focus on a few portraits and success stories to bring major characters alive.

One astonishing example of transplanting the unique product from France was that of hat making, formerly in Caudebec and later in Wandsworth. The secret of the liquid composition used in preparing rabbit hair and beaver skins was lost to France for forty years. Ironically, during that time, Protestant England provided the red hats worn by French Catholic cardinals. The most popular biscuit maker became Le Mann, near the Royal Exchange. The best maker of telescopes was John Dollond (1706–1761) of Huguenot stock, who, by combining the use of five or six separate lenses, enabled telescopes to reproduce more distant, as well as clearer, images.

Some indication of the ingenuity of Huguenot manufacturers arises from the record of their inventions in the English Patent Rolls. England had early on welcomed talent from overseas. These immigrants had improved the manufacture of silks, velvets, brocades, wool, linen, lace, stockings and new modes of dyeing, sailcloth, sacking, paper for bank notes, upholstery, fur-hats, sugar-refining, metal construction of blades, buckles, pins and needles, scythes, cutlery, silver and gold jewelry, in addition to carpets, boots, ceramics, clocks, guns, and looking glasses.

Agnew provides an excellent summary of the novelties that the French Protestant manufacturers of England supplied to the United Kingdom. He shows that the French refugees introduced the art of calico-printing and wax-bleaching, weaving of gin for beautifying ruffs and woollen products and raising the nap on cloth. Some inventions are recorded and can, therefore, be dated accurately. In 1693, Thomas Savery, an engineer, obtained the patent for a steam machine that would pump water from the mines. In 1698, Francis Pousset found the art of making black and white silk crepe. Three years later, Richard Laurence de Manoir and Lewis Anne Sainte Marie obtained a patent for an engine that created large rough-looking glass-plates and chimney-pieces. In 1715, Peter Dubison invented a way of printing, dyeing, or staining calicoe fabrics. In 1719, James Christopher Le Blon is credited with the invention of multiplying pictures and draughts by a natural collotype. In 1720, John Théophilus Désaguliers and others started using steam to create energy and a machine to cure smoky chimneys, while Isaac de La Chaumette, who also worked on the latter project, invented a cannon-piece of ordnance. In 1723, Néhémiah Champion discovered a method of increasing the production of brass from copper and calamy. In 1727, James Christopher Le Blon invented a loom used in making tapestry . . .

This survey is useful to indicate the fields in which the French innovators were strongest—cloth and engineering. The totality of inventions indicates that the English recognized their talents and rewarded them.[1]

A few inventors deserve special consideration. Jean Théophilus Désaguliers was an itinerating public lecturer and brilliant scientist and inventor whose story deserves recalling. He was responsible for the first air-conditioning system in the House of Commons and for the Planetarium; he also invented the safety valve. He became a Fellow of the Royal Society as did James Six, another Huguenot who invented a thermometer capable of recording minimum and maximum temperatures obtained during the absence of any observer.

His father was a theologian of the church of Aytre near La Rochelle. Exiled to Guernsey and having repaired to England, he was ordained in the Anglican Church in 1692. He served a first parish at Swallow-Street and then founded a school at Islington where he remained until his death. His son, John Théophilus, left La Rochelle at two years of age and lived in England until he died, in 1744. His father was his only teacher, so he helped him in turn by teaching at Islington, while he devoted his spare time to his passion for mathematics and science. After his father's death, John Théophilus felt free to apply to Oxford. He gained his B.A. degree in 1709 and, henceforth, devoted his life to science. He was so admired that, at the young age of twenty-seven, he was called to replace professor Keil in the Chair of Natural Philosophy at Oxford.

Having been ordained, he was made chaplain to the Duke of Chandos and then to the Prince of Wales. He was then introduced to the London society of scientists, became a Fellow of the Royal Society in 1714 and was invited to teach Experimental philosophy—lectures that George II and his wife Caroline attended faithfully. He then replaced Robert Hooke after the latter's death and gave public lectures on physics. He helped with the experiments of the aging Newton and propagated his ideas in London and Holland. He himself, among other works, invented a machine called the planetarium, which served to determine the exact distances of the heavenly bodies according to the systems of Newton and Copernicus. The Académie of Bordeaux awarded him its prize for the best essay on electricity.[2]

Huguenots were, therefore, responsible for inventions of great consequence. Thomas Savery's machine to drain mines could also be used to bring water to towns; but to bring water at a higher level, one needed pressure; one could not use more than 3 atmospheres, and Savery's machine had no safety valve.[3] In 1698, Savarin also obtained a patent for a machine for draining marshes, which helped agriculture. The invention of the safety valve, however, was the work of Denis Papin.

Denis Papin was born in 1647 at Blois into a family of doctors and theologians, which became divided by religious confession. He died at Marburg in 1714. A student of medicine and philosophy, he went to England to study physics under R. Boyle through whom he was elected to a fellowship of the Royal Society. After the Revocation, he first went to Hesse, in Germany and received a mathematical chair at Marburg. Yet, the German Academy of Science failed to elect him as a member for his invention of a machine that measured atmospheric pressure. It was warmly welcomed by the Royal Society of London in 1687. He imagined the safety valve in 1681 and, in 1687, created the piston-valve. He applied the use of steam to the propulsion of ships and wrote his findings in a treatise, *The art of rendering water very useful by the aid of fire.* In 1707, he attempted to carry out the idea of the steamship on the river Fulda, but was stopped by jealous German mariners, worried about the future of their profession. Papin also invented the first pressure cooker, and a new digester, which could extract all the nutritious matter from animal bones, hitherto rejected as useless.[4] In his diary, Evelyn reports a supper given for the Fellows of the Royal Society, which was successfully prepared by Papin's digester.

A family of Huguenots kept the secret of the mid-wifery forceps for five generations. They were the Chamberlens. Peter Chamberlen the Elder, who died in 1631, was the son of a Huguenot who had left Paris in 1569 and had found shelter in Protestant Southampton. A celebrated "accoucheur", he, in that capacity, attended the queens of James I and Charles I. He was the first of his family to use the short midwifery forceps. This instrument consisted of two distinct blades which, when placed together, held the foetal head as between two hands, which could be put into place separately and could then be interlocked at the handle end of the blades, and used together as an instrument of traction. The family kept it a secret through part of the eighteenth century.[5]

Much later, the Peter Mark Roget of Huguenot stock and *Thesaurus* fame produced a greatly improved slide-rule. He was secretary of the Royal Society from 1827 to 1849.

In Charlestown, South Carolina, an inventor produced a pendulum engine for pounding the wild rice, so that it lost useless material and thus reduced the cost of threshing, winnowing, and husking rice. His name was Peter Jacob Guerard. He received the patent in 1691, eleven years after reaching North America.[6]

France lost not only some of its inventors but also many manufacturers. France was not totally oblivious to the loss it would suffer from the departure of its valuable Huguenot contributors. In fact, the renowned General Vauban wrote a memorandum to Louis XIV concerning the desirability of recalling the Huguenots to France. He naturally deplored that the military force of France had suffered—the navy had lost eight thousand to nine thousand sailors and the army ten thousand to twelve thousand soldiers with five hundred to six hundred officers.[7] He correctly estimated that the monarch had lost eighty thousand to one hundred thousand subjects through flight, that they had taken much hard cash with them, that many artisans had fled, damaging French commerce, and that some manufacturing techniques, previously a French monopoly, were now abroad to the detriment of French exports.[8]

Gunmakers, for instance, in the time of Louis XIV, set higher standards in the design and the finish of firearms. Two leading Parisian gunmakers who found refuge as Huguenots in London were Pierre Monlon and Pierre Gruche. Monlon was appointed in 1689 as Gentleman Armourer in Ordinary to King William III. Two others were Noël de Landreville and Jacques Gorge; the former produced a light sporting rifle with double action, allowing firing in quick succession; the latter invented a gun with separate chambers linked to a single barrel by a curved connecting passage.[9]

On the lighter note of apparel, one of the most important innovations was the creation of new draperies made from mixed fabrics. These were lighter and softer and therefore excellent for export to Southern Europe and other warmer climates. In the New York colony, 13 percent of French emigrants were also in the cloth and leather trades.[10]

The reduction in the number of manufacturers and their workmen in France resulting from immigration was, indeed, disastrous for the economy of the realm. France was renowned for the whiteness and quality of its paper products. The manufacturers in Ambert in Auvergne fled with their artisans and the factories of Angoumois were reduced from sixty to sixteen working mills.

In Touraine, there were four hundred tanneries, but only fifty-four remained in 1698. The two thousand four hundred bales of silk used in manufactures were reduced to eight hundred. Of the eight thousand looms for making silk stuff, only twelve hundred remained. The seven hundred silk mills were reduced to seventy, and of the approximately forty thousand workmen employed in reeling and manufacturing the silk, only four thousand remained. Only sixty of the three thousand ribbon mills were left.

Of the eighteen thousand looms for making all types of textiles that had been employed in Lyon in 1698, about four thousand remained, as both masters and artisans had gone abroad. The vacancies in Normandy were striking because more than twenty-six thousand habitations were left deserted. Normandy's chief product was fine linen, which was also manufactured in Brittany. In and around Paris, the manufacturers of gold and silver lace as well as of jewelry and fashions, left in great numbers, as they were mainly of the Reformed faith.

The province of Champagne had eighteen hundred and ten looms, but only half of them remained. In Rethel, only thirty-eight of the original eighty woolen factories were left. In Méziers, of one hundred and nine looms for the manufacture of serge, only eight remained. Sedan also suffered greatly. In the villages of Givonne and Daigny, which were employed in the making of iron products, sixty makers of stoves, scythes, and other utensils, emigrated within a month. In Brittany, the trade in fine linen conducted in Landerneau, Brest, and Morlaix, decreased by two thirds, and the manufacture of sail-cloth in Rennes, Nantes and Vitré was reduced so rapidly that the peasants ceased to grow hemp. In Maine, out of twenty thousand workers, only approximately six thousand remained, including women and children who spun and reeled. They were producers of fine linen.[11]

Not only the reduction in the number of manufacturers and workers in France, but also the importation money saved by the English are proof of the general accuracy of General Vauban's analysis. Sailcloth had previously been imported to England from Normandy and Brittany, and, in 1669 England had paid £171,000 for its importation. The same area of France produced white linens, and England's import from one port alone amounted to 4,500,000 livres in charges.

Painted linens were first manufactured in England in 1690 and became a source of England's wealth. Until 1686, England had produced only coarse and dark paper, but the French refugees taught England to make pure white paper, and this was particularly valuable for banknotes.[12] According to MacPherson the exportation from France to England was greatly diminished from the years from 1683 to 1723. In a year silk imports cost £600,000 less; in all types of sailcloth and flax £500,000 less; in beaver hats, watches, clocks and glassware £ 222,000 less; paper costs were reduced by £90,000; hardware, by £40,000; plain fabrics, by £150,000; French wines, by £200,000 and brandies by £80,000;—in all a total of £1,882,000 saved per annum in British imports. All that was the gift of the Huguenots to England.[13]

In the Channel Isles, the French refugees inaugurated the manufacture of stockings and woolen waistcoats, the latter so aptly named 'Jerseys.'

Scotland and Ireland also served as refuge for the Huguenots. Walloons had settled in Edinburgh's Canongate in 1605. They and others taught the Scots the cultivation and preparation of flax for making yarns. By 1707, records show that over four hundred Huguenot families had settled in Scotland. Most of them earned their livings as spinners and weavers of linen silk and worsted.

The Huguenots also introduced to Scotland new agricultural products and techniques—vegetables and flowers, including Brussels sprouts, carrots, cauliflower, and beets, as well as tulips and lilacs. They had also taught the Dutch to grow roses, carnations, and honeysuckle; and the Dutch were not long in outstripping their teachers. The refugees also taught the Scots to lay out fields divided by hawthorn hedges, walls, and fences, and to select better grain for growing grass.

Huguenots made also important contributions to Ireland. The most famous gardens in Ireland were those of Pontarlington which was settled by the second Marquis de Ruvigny as a colony for disbanded French soldiers. Houses were built, resembling those of France and the gardens included small orchards of Italian walnut trees and of Jargonelle pears, under which bees hummed around their hives and women with wide-brimmed straw hats hoed and planted.[14]

A stranger visiting Pontarlington in 1722 is said to have brought with him "Esparagus, radishes, ramolas, sensitive plants, several sorts of letices and about sixty sorts of flower seeds, leamon or citrus trees, ypaticas [hepaticas], orange trees and mhirtle [myrtle] balls in pots clipped into topiary balls and turnip seeds."[15]

Among the wine merchants in Ireland were listed J.C. Raboteau, Pierre le Clerc, Daniel Guyon, and Raymond Pennète. Waterford operated most of the foreign wine trade and also produced the famous Waterford glass. It also manufactured linen, as did Lisburn. Invited by William III, who encouraged the Irish linen trade and discouraged their woolen trade, the most prominent figure of the Irish linen trade became the Huguenot Louis Crommelin.

Born in May 1652 at Armandcourt near St. Quentin, in the province of Picardy, Samuel Louis Crommelin descended from a family of landowners and flax-growers. His father was wealthy, had gone over to the Catholic Church in 1683, but guilt-ridden for having abjured, he returned to his original faith. He left for Amsterdam with his son and two daughters. Having saved much of his fortune, he became a partner in a bank. Later, his two brothers, Samuel and William joined him.

Meanwhile, many Huguenot linen-workers had been invited to Lisburn in Ireland. In 1696, an Act of Parliament had invited Huguenots to settle there and admitted all products of hemp and flax tax-free from Ireland to England. William III then persuaded Crommelin to leave Holland and become Overseer of the Royal Linen Manufacture of Ireland at Lisburn in the autumn of 1698. Louis invited his three brothers. His success became evident. He was even able to require £60 for the hiring of a French minister, Charles Lavalade, whose sister had married his brother Alexander. He died there, at aged seventy-five, on July 14, 1727, and was buried, as were other Huguenots, in the eastern corner of the Cathedral Church.[16]

Other Irish manufacturers included the weavers Le Roux, Latore, Dezouch, James Digue, La Touche, Latigue, Ozier, and Angier. Woolen drapers numbered Alexandre Pellissier and Peter Lunel. Du Bédat was the founder of a sugar refinery.

Dublin and Cork encouraged the settling of Huguenot pewterers, silversmiths, and goldsmiths. Two pewterers in Dublin were James Andouet and Bertrand Piggannet. Goldsmiths and watchmakers included Soret, Benjamin Racine, John Pallet, Noah Vialès, Isaac d'Olier, Jérémiah d'Olier, Thomas de Limarest, Daniel Onge, and James Vidouse. Claude Duplaix manufactured gold and silver lace.

After considering the variety of the manufactures that were brought into Britain by the French Protestant refugees, it is time to address the more famous figureheads of the manufactured products that England no longer had to import. Eventually, the bankers and insurance leaders who assisted them will also be considered.

Possibly the largest manufacturing contribution of the Huguenots to Britain was in the form of textiles—dress accessories and especially silks. The lace manufacturers included Andrew Chaigneau and the fanmakers, Francis Chassereau, who occasionally used ivory. Portraits were even woven out of textiles, as, for example, by Danthon and by Jacques Christophe Le Blon who made a Head of Christ.

From 1670 to 1770, the Huguenots played a major role in the silk industry of London. The most distinguished designers were also Huguenots; the best of them was James Léman. They made every type of elegant silk—black, plain, fancy, and flowered. Black silks were important when rules of mourning were strictest; a secret process including stretching, heating and cosating the warp before weaving imparted extra gloss. In 1688, a patent for the manufacture of lustrings was granted to Paul Cloudesley, William Shérard, and Peter de Cloux. The highly esteemed figured silks manufactured in London at the end of the seventeenth century were products of three refugees, Lanson, Mariscot, and Monceux. Their designer was the Huguenot Christopher Baudoin. John Vansommer was another outstanding designer of figured silks.

The Courtauld family were Huguenot refugees at first, working as goldsmiths during the first eight decades of the 18th century. The family then switched to silk through a marriage link with the Ogiers. Later, they worked in rayon—the first man-made fiber—between 1898 and 1905. The result was that by 1940, Courtaulds dominated the viscose and cellulose acetate processes.[17]

Huguenot goldsmiths and silversmiths were attracted to England because in 1686, in order to finance the wars with Holland Louis XIV demanded that all plate in France be melted down and forbade its future use. There was no further employment for them in France. Refugee goldsmiths and silversmiths came to England from such provincial towns as

Lille, Le Mans, Metz, and Rouen. They introduced a new technique for cast silver to replace the former embossed work, as well as intriguing new shapes in their work, such as the pilgrim bottle, the *écuelle* (a two-handled shallow bowl), sauceboats, and cup-shaped containers for salt in addition to wine-coolers, tankards, sugar-bowls, and, eventually tea-canisters. The two outstanding makers of rococo silver in the 1730s and 1740s were the Huguenots Paul Crespin and the famous Paul de Lamérie.

In the 1690s earlier workers in silver gilt were Pierre Harache the Elder, who devised helmet-shaped ewers and tea-bowls, while Pierre Harache the Younger created pilgrim bottles (that is, wine bottles for display). Peter Archambo prepared a most unusual silver wine-fountain in 1728 for the second Earl of Warrington. It weighed 557 ounces, with two boar handles having superimposed Warrington coats of arms, with a coronet on the top.[18] David Willaume of London made fine silver Communion plate. One example was made for the Church at Pontarlington and ordered by Wilhemina, Princess of Wales. Other renowned goldsmiths were Daniel Garnier, Pierre Platel (whose apprentice was Paul de Lamérie), Louis Cuny and Jean Cartier.

Clocks and watchmakers were legion after 1680 in London. The De Baufré family of Paris developed Nicolas Facio's invention of the jeweled movement in watches, which they patented in 1702. The other leading watchmakers were the Fonnereaus of Ipswich and Simon de Charmes of Hammersmith. Other were also well-known: David Lestourgeon, Peter and Jacob Dehaufré, the brothers Henry and Jacob Massey, and Thomas Grignion who made pierced and engraved watchcases of great elegance.[19]

Engravers helped to personalize jewelry and watchcases by inscribing them. In the 1680s and 1690s, jewelers and watchcase makers used Simon Gribelin's patent-books published in London. From 1705 to 1728, John Obrisset produced a large choice of boxes in horn and tortoise shell planned as tobacco containers. He also designed a horn portrait plaque of Charles I of England and one of Queen Anne. Another distinguished artist was David Le Marchand who made ivory medallion portraits of Samuel Pepys, the diarist, the Duke of Marlborough, Sir Christopher Wren, and the Huguenot Matthew Raper, who became a director of the Bank of England. Others promoting elegant jewelry were the shopkeepers, Paul Daniel Chénevix and Thomas Harrache who also provided Dresden China and bronze statuettes. Their address was at the Golden Ball and Pearl, in Pall Mall.

Many Huguenots of the second generation had an important influence on the development of porcelain in England at Derby and Chelsea. At the latter, Nicholas Sprimont used other Huguenot workmen for models and clock-movements, as porcelain clocks became the fashion. Sauceboats, saltcellars, and porcelain surrounds for clocks were often made with soft paste porcelain. One of the best known decorators of porcelain was James Giles.[20]

Because Huguenots were excluded from printing or selling books, they repaired to England, Holland, or America to continue their livelihood. About two thirds of printers' journeymen, for example, had at least rudimentary reading and writing ability, and were attracted, like their masters, to Protestantism.[21] Already in the late sixteenth century, Thomas Vautrollier had settled in London and printed Latin and English editions of Calvin's *Institutes*. François Vaillant, who had been a bookseller for the Protestant academy at Saumur, opened a bookstore in the Strand in 1686. His shop remained in family ownership for almost eighty years.

Bookbinders also repaired to England and made a name for themselves, which was passed on through successive generations. Queen Victoria and the Prince and Princess of Wales for instance, appointed Robert Rivière, of Huguenot ancestry, as a restorer of ancient books and bindings. He bound the first edition of the major works of Coleridge the poet. Huguenots also introduced new experiments in color printing and improved the quality of white paper.[22] It was Henry Portal, a pupil of Gérard de Vaux who established his own mill in 1712. By 1724, he was manufacturing the paper on which the Bank of England Notes were printed.[23]

Penrose St. Amant speaks of the strong element of vitality in early Huguenot history:

> The discoveries and inventions of these gifted people came into general use throughout the South. The newspaper, printing and bookbinding business of South Carolina was controlled by French Protestants for an extended period in the 18th century. They were leaders in what was perhaps the first fire insurance company in Charleston, organized in 1735. The virtues of thrift, frugality, diligence, discipline, patience, hard work, and a sense of destiny which were rooted in their Calvinistic heritage, persisted in Huguenot life long after the heritage had been widely secularized. Enthusiasm and serenity persisted.[24]

Daniel Marot's designs had a strong impact on furniture making during the first two decades of the eighteenth century. His engravings were published; the Pelletier family used them as did James Pascall, who prepared rococo furniture for the Temple Newsam House in Leeds, the home of Henry the seventh Viscount Irwin. In 1700 Jean Pelletier carved four gilt frames for marble tables and six pairs of large stands, all for Hampton Court Palace. Among the well-to-do, the combination of walnut wood and gilt framing was highly popular.[25]

Refugees from Chatellerault brought ironwork to Boston as a specialty. Apollos Rivoire from Guernsey became a goldsmith in Boston; his son was Paul Revere. In the Carolinas, two goldsmiths and silversmiths were Solomon Legaré de Longuemare and his son Nicholas. They made silver and brass seals, brass weights, spoons and forks, and wedding rings. His Charleston shop sold hemp, rum, oil, and hoes.

The English promoters of colonization by the French in South Carolina, the Lord Proprietors of London, had accepted the proposal of two Huguenot refugees, René Petit and Jacob Guérard to settle eighty family refugees in the colony who were skilled in the manufactures of silks, oils and wines. They were to cultivate the vine, olives and silkworms. Although silkworms were imported, these agricultural ventures did not succeed. Here, Barbarians and Royalists vied for supremacy and cared little about the Reformed faith, so that the Huguenot colonists were in Elysian slavery. The pamphlets attracted lay people rather than ministers to the colony, which lacked permanent Reformed ministers until the 1680s. This was thus the land of merchandizing with less than adequate spiritual guidance, which might explain the fact that they, who had fled from oppression, traded in and owned slaves. The principal successful cultivations were those of rice, indigo, and cotton.[26]

The last decade of the seventeenth century was a period of immense commercial expansion. English Huguenots made the very best of their opportunities. This was the epoch of banks, stocks, and shares as well as novel credit instruments. The richest of the merchants were also members of the Consistory of the oldest French Church in Threadneedle Street, in London. In the final years of their century, they included Etienne Seignoret, a silk merchant who was worth approximately £90,000 and David Bosanquet, who left over £100, 000 on his death. There were about twenty other members of the Consistory, each with assets of over £5,000.

Other prosperous businessmen who provided economic assistance were Pierre Alvert, a wine merchant who contributed £7,000 to the New East India Loan of 1698, Jean Esselbroun, the provider of a turnover of cloth imports to Near Europe of £6,900 in 1695–96, and Jacques de Fay, who subscribed £5,600 in government securities and £2,800 of the Bank of England. There were also Louis Gervase the Younger, a strong founder of the Royal Lustrings Company in 1692 and Daniel Jumineau whose turnover in 1695-96 included nearly £3,000 in imports of currants, ginger, and sugar. The latter gained over £1,000 in exporting drapery and leather goods to Europe. René Baudoin's turnover in 1695-96 included over £9,000 in drapery exports and over £7,000 in imports of silk and cochineal. In 1709, he subscribed £6,800 to the doubling of the capital of the Bank of England, and also held £14,187 in East India stock. All these commercial leaders were first generation Huguenot refugees.[27]

Huguenot merchants paid substantial subscriptions to the Bank of England in the 1690s. Seven of the original twenty-four Founding Directors of the Bank of England were of Huguenot or Walloon descent. They included Sir John Houblon, who subscribed £10,000 and became governor of the Bank and, eventually, lord mayor of London. James and Abraham, his brothers, were also directors of the Bank of England, as well as John Lordell, James Denew, Théodore Jansen, and Samuel Lethieullier. The leading Huguenot banker in Ireland was Digges La Touche, the head of a private bank. His son David became the first governor of the Bank of Ireland founded in 1783.

Huguenots, such as the Loubiers also became involved in the growing business of insurance. Several generations of the Bosanquet family were Directors of the Royal Exchange Assurance, and several members of the Minets headed the London Assurance Company. In addition, Huguenots provided 15 percent of the Proprietors and held 15 percent of the first public issue of the London Assurance Company.[28] It is interesting to recall that the poorest artisans, soon after their arrival in London, formed their own "Friendly Society" for amity as well as for financial protection.

In the New World, the de Lanceys, Faneuils, and Droilhets became leading merchants after arriving in New York City and Boston. In Boston, the brothers Faneuil enjoyed extraordinary success as shipowners and traders. Andrew Faneuil was so rich that, on his funeral day, he had three thousand pairs of gloves distributed as well as three hundred rings given to his friends. His nephew Pierre had a building erected to commemorate him. It still serves as a market place or meeting place in Boston.

Philip L'Anglais, known as Philip English, became a renowned ship outfitter. He dealt in spices coming from the Antilles. His tempestuous temperament and candid speech hampered him at the time of the Salem trials. He was arrested in 1692, but escaped to New York. He displayed a spirit of true forgiveness by sending food to Salem, which experienced a shortage in 1693, and the citizens welcomed him back.

Gabriel Bernon, the shipbuilder from La Rochelle, was a tycoon. He was a descendant of Jean Bernon who had embraced Protestantism in 1577 and headed the civilian guard in La Rochelle. Benjamin Bernon,

The Contributions of Huguenot Manufacturers

another family member, was an alderman in La Rochelle in 1619. During the time of the Church of the Desert, meetings were held secretly at his house. Alexander Bernon was a high marine officer in 1672 and probably joined the Catholics, as he led missions in 1688 and 1706 for France. Nevertheless, he died in prison in 1742. Gabriel's father was a merchant who traded with the Antilles. Incarcerated on October 31, 1685, he was released in May 1686, managed to pass his money to Amsterdam, fled France and finally arrived in London in February of 1687.

Gabriel, therefore, went first to Holland and later to London. He was asked by the Society for the Propagation of the Faith among the Indians to prepare to colonize the land at New Oxford in Wisconsin. He paid passage for his wife, some nephews, and forty other people—including their minister—to America, where he founded New Oxford in 1688. Thereafter, he proceeded to develop a skin trade, and was later granted a patent from 1693 to 1696 from the English navy to organize a merchant navy that would ensure communication between Pennsylvania, Virginia, the Antilles, Canada, and New England. At New Oxford, however, his principles caused him to oppose the English who were selling rum to the Indians. He therefore lost the market and the colony in 1713, but changed trade by dealing with the resin and the tar that the English needed for their boots. He was known in Providence, Rhode Island, for the lavishness of his house, and died at ninety-one after having remarried at sixty-seven and having fathered four other children.[29]

An unintended tribute to the industry and commercial success of the English Huguenots is provided in an anonymous pamphlet that appeared in 1775 in London entitled *"Considerations on the mischiefs that may arise from granting too much indulgence to foreigners."* It refers to the French refugees in the following passage:

> As the French are of all people the most enterprising, the most industrious and frugal, so we have the more Reason to be jealous of their Designs and to provide against their Admission into the places of Power, Profit, or Trust. For considering their Frugality, Oeconomy, and Industry, they will in time head all the proffitable [sic] Branches of Trade as they have already have that of the Silk Manufacture, for I believe it can be demonstrated, that nine parts in ten of that Traffick is in their hands, with a great share of that of Wines. Nor are they less considerable with regards to their Numbers . . . And considering their Sobriety and Diet, and the Fruitfulness of their Women, the City, in Time, will probably be called a 'French Colony'

The conclusion of Robin Gwynn's illuminating volume, *Huguenot Heritage* states more positively what the preceding anonymous critic had asserted negatively. Here is Gwynn's tribute:

One is impressed by not only their combination of faith, resolution, and endurance, but also their potentially profitable connections, their need as refugees to apply themselves to whatever they undertook, and consequently their exceptional degree of motivation; the liquid capital and the new craft, skills and techniques they brought with them; their preparedness to experiment and, (if need be), to migrate anew and start again. Given good fortune, such qualities could be turned to profitable account, and we have seen that this is precisely what happened. In the process, not only the refugees, but also the society in which they came benefited hugely, to the great detriment of France. The history of the Huguenots in England shows that the right of a minority to exist is more than moral rule. It is also, as Philippe Joutard remarked, "the most certain means of enriching a civilization and increasing its dynamism."[30]

Notes

1. D.C.A. Agnew, *Protestant exiles*, vol.2, 256.

2. See Smiles. *Huguenots in England and Ireland* (London, 1880), 245–46 and Didot, *Nouvelle biographie générale*. (Paris, 1855). Vol. 13, 722–24. His works included *Fires improved; being a new method of building chimneys, so as to prevent their smoking* (London, 1716). He also wrote sermons, a poem on the Newtonian system, and translated French works from Gauger and Mariotte, among others.

3. As a youth, Savery had lived in a mining district and knew of the great difficulty experienced in keeping mines free from water. He eventually invented a machine for raising water, which, although not a steam engine in the modern sense of the word, embodied the first practical application of the force of steam for mechanical purposes. He wrote an account of it in 1702, in a book entitled *The Miner's Friend*.

4. On inventors, see also Roland Mousnier, *Histoire générale des civilizations*, (Paris: P.U.F., 1967), vol.4, 350.

5. *Dictionary of National Biography*, vol. 4, 14v., and Aveling, *The Chamberlens and the Midwifery Forceps* (London), 215–226.

6. *Transactions of the Huguenot Society of South Carolina*, vol. 96, 43.

7. George A. Rothrock, *The Huguenots: A Biography of a Minority*, (Chicago: Nelson Hall: 1979), 139f.

8. According to an eyewitness, Jacques Fleury, who was a minister at Jussy, it also affected French imports such as wheat, which usually traveled between Geneva and the county of Gex. See his *Journal, 1675–1692*, (Genève: 1994), 124–25. Louis XIV, through Colbert, applied numerous pressures on the counties of Switzerland to force them to return the refugees. But the Swiss were good at dispersing them in boats over Lake Léman to other parts of Switzerland or toward Brandenburg. See 131–32.

9. Murdoch, *The Quiet Conquest*, 223 ff.

10. Joyce D. Goodfriend, *"Too great a mixture of Nations"*, *The Development of New York City Society in the 17th century*, (Ph.D.dissertation at Los Angeles: 1975), 146–47. She also notes that French merchants made up 17 percent of the population and French mariners 19.5 percent, but does not indicate that those would be uniquely Huguenots.

11. W. H. Foote, *The Huguenots or French Reformed Church* (Richmond, Va.: Presbyterian Committee for Publication, 1870), 456 ff.

12. W. H. Foote, *Huguenots*, 406.

13. David MacPherson, *Annals of Commerce*, (London: Nichols and Son, 1805), Vol.2, 609.

14. John Stocks Powell, *Huguenots, Planters*, (Pontarlington: French Church Press: 1994).

15. Ruth Duthie, "The introduction of plants to Britain in the 16th and 17th centuries by strangers and refugees." in *P.H.S.L.*, vol. 24, 403–404.

16. G. E. Reaman, *The trail of the Huguenots in Europe, in the United States, South Africa and Canada*, (London and Baltimore: Genealogical Publications, 1963), 89–95. See also *Dictionary of National Biography*, (London: Oxford University Presses, 1917), vol.5, 145b–146b.

17. Murdoch, *Quiet Conquest*, 306 ff.

18. Murdoch, *Quiet conquest*, 235–242.

19. Murdoch, *Quiet Conquest*, 243–250.

20. Murdoch, *Quiet Conquest*, 255 ff.

21. Abraham D. Lavender, *French Huguenots*, 62.

22. In Boston, three brothers Faneuil, Jean, Benjamin and André wanted to create a paper factory.

23. Murdoch, *Quiet Conquest*, 175–180.

24. Penrose Saint Amant, "Some reflections on Huguenot History" *Transactions of the Huguenot Society of South Carolina*, Vol.91, 57–60.

25. Murdoch, *Quiet Conquest*, 289–304.

26. A. H. Hirsch, *The Huguenots of Southern Carolina*, (Durham, N. C.: Duke University Press: 1928), 15. and Butler, John. *Huguenots in America*, (Cambridge, Mass: Harvard University Press, 1983), 53.

27. Gwynn, *Huguenot Heritage*, 151 ff.

28. Gwynn, *Huguenot Heritage. The History and contributions of Huguenots in Britain*, (London: Routledge and Kegan Paul: 1985), 87.

29. George Chinard, *Les Réfugiés Huguenots*, 96–97.

30. Gwynn, *Huguenot Heritage*, 175. The final sentence of this passage, and the book itself, concludes with this sentence: "At a time when there are more refugees than ever before in human history, yet when governments all around the world are setting up barriers against immigration, the reminder is salutary."

Chapter 7

Huguenot Artists and Architects

Huguenot architects and artists in the realm of both visual and auditory arts also found protectors abroad. Art in the Academies of Paris was very much a matter of collaboration among artists—the master did not work alone but engaged an entire school of artists who executed the work. Artists were also known to collaborate on a piece. This was particularly true in the great palaces, where the portraitist might paint his picture on the wall, while the great trompe-l'oeil artist would do the ceiling and the specialist in history scene would decorate some walls. Until 1681, when Protestant artists were expelled, the two religious confessions of France habitually worked collaboratively. It is an exaggeration, however, to claim as one article does "That in a period of about eighty years linking the end of the reign of Henry IV and those of Louis XIII and XIV up to the fatal date of 1685, we count no less than two to three hundred names, of whom a good number shine in the archives of painting, sculpture, engraving, and architecture of the period."

There seem to be very few records about refugee Huguenot musicians, although music at the court of Charles II was strongly influenced by the French style. Louis Bourgeois, the musical composer for Marot's *Psalms*, remained in France. Louis Grabu was appointed as composer to Charles II, but little has been written about his religious beliefs. Yet, his life reflects the familiar pattern of Huguenot emigration. He remained in England from 1665 to 1679, went back to France until 1683, at which date, he finally returned to England.[1]

The most distinguished Huguenot artists in France included the painter Jean Cousin, the architect Jacques du Cerceaux, the sculptor Jean Goujon, and the potter Bernard Palissy. The greatest architect in the age of Henry IV was Salomon de Brosse who built the palace of Luxembourg for Marie de Medicis, where another Protestant, Jacques Boyceau designed the gardens.

In 1648, the Académie Royale de Peinture was established. Twenty-three of its members (approximately one third) were Huguenots. Among the founding members were Jacques-Samuel Bernard, Louis Ferdinand Elle the elder and Henri Testelin. The Testelins, who were brothers, served as the first two secretaries of the Académie. The elder, Louis, specialized in decorative painting and was commissioned to paint murals for Richelieu's palace. Protestant artists in the Academy included Abraham Brosse, the engraver of views of Paris, the Elles, father and son, both fashionable portrait painters, Jacques Samuel Bernard, a miniaturist who was also an engraver and painted still life, and Jean Michelin, an imitator of the Le Nain brothers, who painted street scenes. Protestant artists were expelled from the Academy in 1681. Jacques-Samuel Bernard and Louis-Ferdinand Elle the elder recanted and were reinstalled in 1686. Among those who fled were Rolland Le Fèbvre, who died in London in 1677 and Jean Michelin, who died on the Isle of Jersey in 1696.

Probably the most famous early Protestant artist in the Academy was Sébastien Bourdon. He painted biblical subjects for churches, murals for the hotels of the wealthy, and landscapes as well as portraits. His propensity for depicting Biblical scenes is obvious in the titles of some of his paintings: *Eliézar and Rebecca, Christ and the Samaritan Woman, The meeting of Jacob and Rachel at the Well, Moses Left in the Bulrushes, The Departure of Jacob,* and *Moses and the Daughters of Jethro,* as well as *The Holy Family*.[2] Queen Christina invited this remarkable talent to Sweden in 1652. His daughter remained a faithful Protestant in France, but, upon her second attempt to escape, reached England safely.[3]

With this impressive background, one would have expected the Huguenot refugees in Britain to include a larger number of outstanding artists than actually existed. Britain tended to favor the Dutch in the realm of visual arts. Still throughout the years, it had welcomed important French artists.

Jacques Le Moyne de Morgues was an early Protestant painter and cartographer. A refugee from France, he flourished between 1553 and 1558. In 1564, he depicted Laudonnière's expedition trying to establish the Huguenot settlement in Florida. He specialized in still life and published a pattern book for painters, engravers and embroideries, *La Clef des Champs, pour trouver plusieurs animaux tant bestes qu'oyseaux avec plusieurs fleurs et fruits* (1586).[4]

Whether or not the great English miniaturist Nicolas Hilliard (1547–1619) was a Huguenot is uncertain. Born in Exeter, his miniature technique was similar to that of the French Court and far advanced of that of the English Court. From 1576–78, he visited the French Court and painted for the duke of Alençon. His distinguished pupil, Isaac Oliver, was a Huguenot. Oliver came to England as a child from Rouen in 1568; he died in London in 1617. As Ellis Waterhouse observes, "Alone of painters in Elizabeth's time, Nicholas Hilliard and his pupil and rival Isaac Oliver are worthy to be named as contributors to the age of Shakespeare."[5]

Isaac Oliver also lived in Venice in 1596. His technique was European in its more dramatic use of light and shade and the use of modeling in the round, which Hilliard clearly avoided. According to Ellis Waterhouse: "It is Oliver who gives us the most living portraits of the reign of James I, prefiguring the style of the next generation."[6] In 1604, Oliver was appointed limner to Queen Anne of Denmark and was granted the monopoly of her portraits in miniature as small as those of Prince Henry's. One of his most impressive works was a full-length miniature of the Earl of Dorset.

The art of miniature paintings continued to flourish after him. The D'Agar family—Jacob, the father and his sons Charles and Peter—emigrated to England in 1681. Jacob later went to be a court painter in Copenhagen. Charles Boit had a similarly uprooting life. Although his family had settled in Stockholm when he was born in 1662, in 1690, he settled in London where he worked as court enamellist and produced miniature copies of famous paintings from 1696. After the death of Queen Anne in 1714, he chose to go to Paris, where he was welcomed under the Regency of the Duke of Orléans, despite his remaining a Protestant. He died there in 1727.

Rolland Lefèbvre (1608–79), a native of Saumur, was only briefly in England from 1676 until his death in 1679. He painted portraits and genre paintings, often in a miniature style. His Protestant background did not prevent his producing carnal scenes.[7]

Louis Chéron had a successful, but somewhat mysterious, life. A decorative painter, he won the Prix de Rome twice in 1676 and 1678, painted a Visitation for a Jacobite Convent, was asked by the Guild of Goldsmiths to provide four paintings from the May exhibitions of Notre-Dame in 1687 and 1691. Yet, he chose to become an exile in 1690. He then was patronized by Ralph, Ist Duke of Montagu, for whom he decorated the ceiling of the saloon and staircase at Boughton House, Northants, with the mythological scenes of *The Assembly of Gods* and *The Judgment of Paris*. A denizen in 1703, he painted *The marriage of Charles I* in 1725. He taught drawing in London at Kneller's Academy and founded the School of Drawing at St Martin's Lane where he worked with Roubiliac and Gravelot. He was also active as a book illustrator.[8]

Miniatures could be made on wood, on canvas, or in enamel.[9] Jean Petitot was an enameler, jeweler, and painter, born in Geneva, and later apprenticed to Charles I as an engraver. He painted an image of St George for the Order of the Garter, then did enameled copies of the paintings of Van Dyck and portraits of King Charles I and members of his family. One of his most admired paintings was the portrait of **Rachael de Ruvigny, Countess of Southampton**. At the time of the Revocation, he happened to be in France, having followed the future King Charles into exile. He asked to remove himself to Geneva and was imprisoned in For-l'Evêque. Bossuet was sent to convert him to Catholicism, and finally abjured in 1687 so that he would be permitted to leave the realm, despite strong feelings of guilt. Geneva accepted him upon his escape from France in 1687, probably because he had written a book of prayers and because of his genuine guilt and sorrow.[10]

He and his friend Jacques Bordier, also from Geneva, and a miniaturist specializing in backgrounds, married two Protestant sisters from Blois— Marguerite and Madeleine Cuper. Jacques Bordier, in 1686, became the secret agent of the Genevan government in Versailles. Like the Petitots, he also went to England to serve Charles II.

Jean Petitot, son of Jean Petitot, born in Blois in 1653, was later sent to England to be instructed in limning. In Charenton he married his cousin Madeleine Bordier who eventually died in Geneva. In 1696, he went to England, where he painted in watercolor and enamel in the style of his father. He perfected the new technique of painting with powdered enamel mixed with oils on an enamel background. We do not know whether he returned to Paris as a Protestant, but he died there six years later.

The painting of historical scenes served often as the background of portrait paintings in the seventeenth century. An exemplar was Jean Michelin, born in Langres in 1629, accepted by the Academy in 1660, and expelled in 1681 because of his religion. He first repaired to Germany. There he directed a tapestry manufacture in Hanover from 1668 to 1686, under the patronage of the Duke of Luneberg for whom he had executed a series of miniature portraits. He died on the Isle of Jersey in 1696.

Nicholas Heude, a historical painter, born in Le Mans, was invited to join the Academy in 1673, and fled to England in 1683. He worked as an assistant to Verrio and finally settled in Scotland in 1695, at the invitation of the Duke of Queensberry. His work included two signed ceilings, such as the *Aurora* at Caroline Park near Edinburgh; he died there in poverty in 1707. Pierre Berchet also first came to England as an assistant of Verrio in 1681. He returned to France, despite his Protestant affiliation, worked at Marly for a while, and settled back in England in 1685. Among his other works, he painted *The Ascension* on the ceiling of Trinity College, Oxford, in 1694.

A painter greatly admired by the House of Hanover was Philip Mercier (1689?–1760). He was, like John Van der Bank, the Dutch illustrator of *Don Quixote*, the son of a Huguenot tapestry worker.[11] His father had, however, migrated as a Huguenot to Berlin, where Philip is said to have been born. Coming to London, he painted *Viscount Tyrconnel and His family* as an amusing conversation piece. He included a self-portrait in the picture, whose main topic was depicting others at play, thus following the example of the great French master, Poussin. When Frederick, Prince of Wales, reached England from Hanover, he backed Mercier, his former friend. In 1728, Mercier was appointed painter to the Prince of Wales, then page of the bedchamber and library keeper. He painted full-length portraits of the three princesses and eventually produced a series of portraits of the Prince of Wales.

A brilliant and popular painter at the courts of Louis XIV and William III of England, Jacques Rousseau was born of Protestant parents in Paris in 1630. His gift was *trompe-l'oeil* perspective painting. In the Salon de Venus in Versailles (the great ceremonial stateroom that measured forty feet long and forty-five feet wide), he created vast illusionist paintings. They stretched to the ceiling so that the visitor was momentarily deceived into believing genuine the great vista of palaces, courts, and gardens, gloriously dominating this perspective. There were also two additional vistas opposite the doors of statues of Meleager and Atalanta. Other illusionist perspectives were installed at the Orangerie at Saint Cloud and at the mansion of Marly for the brother of King Louis XIV.[12] The Versailles *trompe-l'oeil* are still in place.

Some tapestry weavers also came to London. Michael Claras Vaux, who had brought some designs from the Gobelins manufacture, stayed briefly. He had worked at Aubusson, where so many weavers were Protestants that, with the exodus, the factory slumbered from 1685 to 1730. Aubusson had warehouses at Avignon, Aix, Nîmes, Montpellier, and Toulon, much of which was Protestant land. Claras Vaux eventually went to Germany where he was better appreciated. Two other refugee tapestry designers and makers, Danthon and Chabeux, have left little record of what they did in England.[13]

London welcomed other Huguenot artists in the eighteenth century such as Balthasar Fellushier, Théodore de la Gardelle (a miniaturist), as well as Jacob Bonneau and Mary de Vilebrun, both of whom exhibited at the Royal Academy in 1772. In 1753, an attempt that ultimately failed was made to inaugurate an Academy of Art, with thirteen distinguished Huguenot participants at the Turk's Head. These included Roubiliac, Moser, the medallist, the distinguished Goujon, and the two Elles.

In Montagu House, Protestant and Catholic painters and decorators worked side by side, as they had in France before the persecutions began. Jacques Parmentier, a pupil of Bourdon, collaborated with Berchet and La Fosse. He died in London in 1730. La Fosse was also a Protestant, as well as Jacques Rousseau, but both worked with a Catholic, the great Monnoyer.

Among the Huguenot artists in Ireland, there were a few talented women, including one named Henrietta Beaulieu, whose first married surname was Dering. She later married a man named Johnston, who went as a missionary to Charleston, South Carolina, in 1702, where she became the first woman painter of America. She died twenty-seven years later. Another woman and a landscapist, Susan Drury, gained a Dublin prize for two paintings of the Giant's Causeway using gouache on vellum.

Ireland also hosted Gabriel Béranger (1729–1817). Born in Amsterdam, he joined his refugee family in 1750 in Dublin; his interest was antiquarian themes in drawings or watercolors. Two brothers, Thomas and Thomas Sautelle Roberts, the best eighteenth century landscape artists in Ireland, were of impeccable Huguenot descent. The most impressive Huguenot cartographer in Ireland was John Rocque "who transformed the Irish estate map from a dull exercise in field surveying to a species of fine art embellished with beautiful topographical views and rococo ornaments." His major works were *London and Its Environments* and *Exact Survey of the City and Suburbs of Dublin*.[14]

There is little to report about early Huguenot artists in North America, except for two painters who produced portraits in the early days in Charleston—Madame La Mer and Jeremiah Theus. The latter painted Jacob Motte, Gabriel Manigault (a famous merchant manufacturer and planter) and his wife, and Madame Prioleau whose husband was descended from a doge of Venice.[15] Huguenot painting, however, continued in America through so-called Sunday painters. Camille Bombois, for instance, was a street paver, Louis Vivin was a postal clerk and Séraphine was a washerwoman. All three produced several paintings for the middle-class of the colonies.

The Beaudoin family was split, as were so many other families. Many Beaudoins remained in England, including the renowned designer of interlaced flowers in silk. Jacques Bowdoin, named after the governor of Massachusetts, founded Bowdoin College in Maine. Actually, it was originally in Massachusetts, but a change of boundaries now locates it in Maine.

Huguenot Sculptors and Carvers

The baroque world loved sculpture, which gave human form to columns, chiaroscuro to buildings, and moral lessons to those walking in gardens. Hubert le Sueur, born in Paris in 1590, was renowned for his technical skill in bronze casting. He had assisted in the casting of the famous statue of Henry IV in Paris. In England, he sculpted a remarkable equestrian statue of Charles I for Trafalgar Square, and the superb tombs of Buckingham and of his Duchess Katherine Manners in Westminster Abbey. He also carved the Fountain of Arethusa, known as the Diana Fountain on the Thames-side garden of Somerset House, the residence of Queen Henrietta-Maria. His friend Maximilian Cote, who came to England in 1596, joined his elder brother Julian, the creator of the funeral effigy carried at the funeral of Mary Queen of Scots. Maximilian was helped by the Cecils. He prepared a Westminster Abbey tomb for the king's little daughters. His finest work is on the tomb of the senior Sir John Denham at Egham.[16]

At the time of the Revocation, Matthew Gosset fled from Normandy to England. He mainly produced wax portraits and statuary at St. Anne's Westminster. Josias Iback became a denizen on June 22, 1694. Little is known about his private life, but he probably came to England, via Bever in Hanover. He is known for his equestrian statue of Charles II at Windsor. Nadauld fled in 1699 and was one of the Earl of Devonshire's protégés. In 1700, he replaced Cibber as a sculptor of stone figures at Chatsworth. His specialty was allegorical chimneypieces and busts. He made a monument at Westminster Abbey to Lady Eland, granddaughter of the French Protestant Marquise de la Tour de Gouvernet. He seems to have worked at Castle Howard from 1709 to his death.

Unquestionably, the most distinguished eighteenth century sculptor in England was Louis-François Roubiliac, who was unrivaled in popularity. He was born in the first decade of the eighteenth century in Lyons and christened in its Catholic Church of St. Niziers in that city. He converted to Protestantism in France and married a Huguenot, Catherine Hélot, at St. Martin's-in-the-Fields in 1735. His surname is of Gascon origin like that of another famous Huguenot, the actor Garrick. He learned sculpture from Balthasar per Moser, then resident in Dresden, a disciple of Bernini and one of his most distinguished followers. Roubiliac later entered Coustou's studio and gained the second grand prix with a sculpture of Daniel saving Susannah at the moment when she was condemned to death. He worked first in England for Thomas Carter who specialized in chimneypieces and later for Henry Chère; he was the friend of many London goldsmiths.

His famous early statue of George Frederick Handel was made from a single block of marble, depicting the composer as Orpheus, playing the lyre, with a boy below him writing down the notes on a score. Handel's face expresses an intense look of concentration. It was set in an arch with figures representing Harmony.

Roubiliac had a gift for characterization in stone. The Dormer monument at Quainton reveals his sense of drama—a dead son lies in his grave clothes with his hands folded on his chest, while the weeping mother kneels at the boy's feet—and the father stands erect.

Roubiliac also produced indefatigably high quality statues and busts, such as that of Sir John Cass. His nephew commissioned the one of Sir Isaac Newton. Garrick, the Shakespearean actor, rejoiced in his eagerness to sculpt Shakespeare as well as the bard's famous interpreter. He made a bust of Alexander Pope and another for his friend Hogarth; he sculpted Dean Swift and the Duke of Marlborough.

Roubiliac reached the peak of his fame with his monument in Westminster Abbey for the second duke of Argyll and Greenwich. This evokes Eloquence, while History aloft bears the book on which are inscribed Argyll's dates, and, at the feet of Liberty, there is a scroll inscribed "Magna Charta." The memorial was flattering to Argyll's gifts of speech and his historical contribution to liberty. Perhaps the subtlest detail is that Eloquence is pictured as having trembling lips. Of the same character was his sepulchral sculpture of the Duke of Montagu, showing Charity erecting a shrine to his memory, applauded by Fame.

Other statues of his commemorated St. John, Viscount Bolingbroke and his Huguenot second wife, the Marchioness of Villette, the Fourth Earl of Chesterfield, as well as Field-Marshal Lord Ligonier who was of Huguenot descent.[17]

He could also produce pieces with larger themes such as the series of *The Temple of the Four Monarchies*. Philip Stanhope, 4th Earl of Chesterfield observed: "Roubiliac only was a statuary, the rest stone-cutters," and in 1771 John Wesley considered that only two tombs at Westminster Abbey, both by Roubiliac, were incomparable—those of Mrs. Nightingale and of General Hargrave. The former is remarkable by its pathos—the husband tries to divert the arrow of death from his wife who is dying in childbirth. The latter shows the dead general standing upright at his resurrection.

From the monumental, we return to the small and delicate. David Le Marchand was the most gifted carver of ivory. Born in Dieppe in 1674, he died in London in 1726. He specialized in portraits, making handsome busts or deeply carved oval medallions and also statuettes. He opened a shop in Edinburgh in 1696; by 1705, he had moved to London. In 1697, he carved a bust in the round of the philosopher John Locke. In 1716, he made the portrait of George I. His most notable achievements were the portraits of Sir Isaac Newton and Sir Christopher Wren. His style was famous for flowing locks of hair and intricately chiseled facial features.

Another impressive carver was Jean Obrisset who worked in horn or tortoise shell. His most renowned productions included the Drake box—depicting Drake's voyages—, images of various sovereigns of England, as well as the Conversion of Paul the Apostle. Jean Cavalier, another ivory carver, portrayed Charles II on horseback in 1684 and produced medallions of Samuel Pepys in 1688 and of William III in 1690.[18]

Other designers of portrait plaques of jewelry and of elegant watchcases included Simon Gribelin, who produced popular pattern books used by jewelers and watchmakers, Peter Parquet, Paul Daniel Chenevix, Thomas Harrache, and Thomas Grignion, as well as Jame Giles, who became renowned as a porcelain decorator.

The three most famous designers of gold and silver were Paul de Lamérie, Paul Crespin, and Nicolas Sprimont. Paul de Lamérie was born in Hertogenbosch in 1668 and died in London in 1751. He was the son of Huguenot parents who emigrated to the Netherlands before settling in London by 1691. Between 1715 and 1749, his flourishing workshop employed as many as thirteen apprentices. Until 1732, his work concentrated on designing silver of the highest quality—95.84 percent purity—, which was termed Britannia silver. He made a pair of winecoolers for Philip Dormer Stanhope, the 4th Earl of Chesterfield. Robert Walpole, first Earl of Orford and Algernon Coote, 6th Earl of Montrath were his patrons. In the 1730s, he was one of the first English silversmiths to work in the rococo style. An inkstand made for Blenheim Palace used his favorite motifs—strapwork, corkscrew spirals, writhing sea serpents, and marine plants—conveying a sense of continuous movement. He was so highly regarded that in 1740, he was commissioned by the goldsmiths' Company for an ewer and dish displaying a variety of silversmithing techniques, with marine decorations of sea-monsters, foam work, winged mermaids, and tritons.[19]

Paul Crespin, an outstanding silversmith, was born in London in 1694, the son of Huguenot refugees who had arrived in 1687. Like de Lamérie, he adopted the rococo style early in the 1730s. His work was appreciated by English aristocrats such as Charles Spencer, the 3rd Duke of Marlborough at Blenheim Palace and Robert Walpole. Crespin made tableware, including centerpieces, two handled cups, tureens and spice-boxes. One of his famous pieces, produced for Charles Seymour 6th Duke of Somerset, was a silver tureen supported on the backs of two goats.

The third major silversmith was Nicolas Sprimont. Born to refugee parents in Liège in 1716, he died in London in 1771. He was also designed notable examples of porcelain. He manufactured centerpieces, tureens, sauce-boats, and saltcellars. He too used the rococo style in both silver and porcelain, and the products of his Chelsea porcelain factory dominated the fashion in English porcelain.

Among a large group of engravers were Paul Foudrinier, Isaac Basire, and François Vivarais. Paul Foudrinier specialized in publishing engravings of architectural plans. Vivares (or Vivarais) was born in St. Jean-du-Bruel in southern France in 1708, arrived in London in 1711, and died there in 1780. He was subsequently recognized as "The Father of English Landscape Engraving." He engraved plates for William de la Cour's *First Book of Ornaments* (1741). Many of his landscape prints were after paintings of French and Dutch Old Masters. He began with nineteen plates for Arthur Pond's *Italian Landscapes* project and went on to a forty-four plate survey of the works of Gaspar Dughet and Claude Lorrain in British Collections and of contemporaries such as Gainsborough and Zuccarelli. A working partnership with Thomas Smith of Derby resulted in twenty-three prints. Their *View of the Upper Works at Colebrookdale* and *South West Prospect of Colebrookdale*, both from 1758, are the earliest surviving depictions of the most important site of the Industrial Revolution. In 1753, he published after his own designs *A View in Craven, Yorkshire*, and *A View of Amazing Rock in Craven, Yorkshire*. From 1750 to 1760, he engraved and published decorative borders for wallpaper use.[20] Vivarais, Rocque, and Chatelain, among others, disseminated the rococo style in England by publishing and engraving the latest Parisian designs.[21]

One individual who forms a liaison between artists and architects is Jean Tijou, an outstanding designer of metal work who collaborated with the architect Daniel Marot. He arrived in England in 1689 as a Huguenot refugee. For the first decade, he worked for William III and Mary II at Hampton Court. He made the wrought iron balustrade and the gates and screen of the Fountain Gardens. He also worked at Chatsworth, Derbyshire, on the balustrades of the interior great stairs and on the balcony stairs on the south front. In 1695, he published his executed designs in *A New Book of Drawings Invented and Designed by Jean Tijou, 1693*. This was the earliest English book on ironwork designs. Tijou also worked at St. Paul's Cathedral under Sir Christopher Wren, in the Chapel of St. Michael and St. George, creating the sanctuary screen, and the guardrail for the landing of the geometrical stair. He revolutionized ironwork in England by emphasizing its decorative potential.

Architecture

Solomon De Caus and Isaac De Caus, born in the sixteenth century, were among the early designers and architects that took refuge in England. Solomon De Caus arrived in 1610 and taught drawing to Henry Prince of Wales. For him, he built a picture gallery in Richmond, and to him he dedicated his first book, *La Perspective*. He included designs for the gardens of the prince in his second book, *Les raisons des forces mouvantes*. He then moved to the Palatinate, where he created his major work, the Castle Garden, *Hortus Palatinus* at Heidelberg.[22]

Isaac De Caus built a grotto in the basement of the Banqueting House in London, designed by Inigo Jones. A leading garden designer for James I and Charles I, he built another grotto for Queen Henrietta-Maria at Somerset House. He was pensioned and given accommodation for life by the Herbert family in gratitude for his modern French style architectural improvement of their Wilton House, which became a model for the rest of the country.[23]

A most important architect, Daniel Marot, the favorite of William III, came with him from the United Provinces and immediately began to work on the gardens and the interior furnishings of Hampton Court. He even designed the king's stagecoach. Marot had a profound impact on England, as a result of the publication of his magnificent set of designs issued at The Hague in 1702. In addition, he invented the new concept that all the furniture in a room should be designed by the same hand, and, if possible, by the architect of the house. The designer architects William Kent and Robert Adam followed this principle very successfully in the eighteenth century.

This gifted architect and designer also worked for the Duke of Montagu at Montagu House in London, where he planned the painting panels for the walls of the state drawingroom. The baskets of fruit were probably painted by Jean-Baptiste Monnoyer, the mythological scenes by Charles La Fosse and the *trompe-l'oeil* picture frames by Jacques Rousseau.[24]

Daniel Marot's engraved designs exerted a strong influence on the furniture produced from 1700 to 1720. Use of them was made by the Pelletier family, and by the notable carver, James Pascall. Pelletier carved four gilt frames for marble tables and six large stands for the Palace of Hampton Court. Pascall carved in gilt, pine, and walnut, eight candle stands for Henry, the seventh Viscount Irwin, for Temple Newsam House, Leeds.

Two other Huguenot architects were Samuel Handuroy and Jean de Bodt who produced designs for Dyrham Park, Avon, and Wentworth Castle in Yorkshire, while Nadauld, a refugee stone carver, worked on ornamental sculpture for the mansions of Chatsworth and Castle Howard. Architects in the early eighteenth century were making impressive use of ornamental or furniture designers, and often copied the vigorous rococo style of France. Even Sir Christopher Wren, at an earlier time, was happy to use the designs of Tijou's A *New Book of Drawings* of 1693 for St Paul's Cathedral, which were also employed at Burghley, Chatsworth, and Hampton Court.[25]

In the colonies, the name that stands out in architecture is that of Pierre Faneuil. His contribution gave Boston the building that was part of a square he had constructed in which the Independence of America from England was freely and rigorously discussed. Hence, Faneuil Hall is regarded as a monument of American liberty.

Conclusion

This survey of Huguenot painters, engravers, sculptors, carvers, and architects indicates that among the numerous contributors were several extremely distinguished individuals. These were the miniaturist Oliver, the sculptors Roubiliac and le Sueur, and the architect Marot. The Huguenot contributions to the military, manufacturing, scientific inventions, librarianship, theology, literature, and medicine were even more impressive.

Notes

1. *B.S.H.P.F.*, (Paris: 1856), vol.4, 6–8 ff. It is, of course, possible that Louis XIV's passion for the arts was such that he was prepared to overlook the Protestant affiliation of some after the exodus of the post-1685s, but this is merely conjecture.

2. These can be seen in various American museums: Boston, Chicago, Houston, and Minneapolis.

3. Menna Prestwich, "Distinguished Protestants in Art and Architecture" in Irène Scouloudi, ed. *Huguenots in Britain and their French Background, 1550–1800*, (London: Macmillan: 1987).

4. *Ibid*.

5. *Painting in Britain, 1530–1790*, 3rd ed. (London: Penguin, 1969), 33. Robert Cecil emphasizes the taste of royalty for miniature paintings. See also Erna Auerbach, *Tudor Artists*, (London: Athlone Press, 1954), 168–69.

6. Ellis Waterhouse, *Painting in Britain*, 45.

7. Waterhouse, *The Dictionary of 16th & 17th century Painters*. (London: Penguin Books, 1958), 169.

8. Henry Manchy, "Huguenot London: The City of Westminster" *P.H.S.L.* vol. 14, 144–90.

9. On French painters and their techniques, see Christopher Wright, *The French Painters of the Seventeenth Century*, (New York: Graphic Society/Little Brown, 1985).

10. "Un grand peintre protestant sous Louis XIV: Jean Petitot" *B.S.H.P.F*, vol. 20, 175 ff.

11. Ellis Waterhouse, *Painting in Britain*, 181 and 189.

12. Elspeth A. Evans, "Jacques Rousseau: A Huguenot Decorative Artist at the Court of Louis XIV and William III" *P.H.S.L.*, vol.20, 142–160.

13. See W. Hefford, "Soho and Spitalfields: Little Known Huguenot Tapestry Weavers in and Around London, 1680–1780." *P.H.S.L*, 103ff.

14. Martin Anglesea, "Irish Artists with Huguenot Backgrounds" in *P.H.S.L.*, vol.26, 69 f.

15. A. H. Hirsch, *The Huguenots of South Carolina*. (Durham, North Carolina: Duke University, 1928), 162.

16. Katheleen A. Esdaile, "The Part played by Refugee Sculptors, 1600–1750." in *P.H.S.L.*, vol.18, 254–262.

17. Information in the preceding paragraphs came from Tessa Murdoch's article, "Louis-François Roubiliac and His Huguenot connections" in *P.H.S.L.*, vol.24, 26–45, and from Kathleen Esdaile's *The life and works of Louis-François Roubiliac*, (London: Oxford University Press: 1928) *Passim*. See also D. Bindmau and M. Baker, *Roubiliac and the Eighteenth century Monument: Sculpture as Theatre*, (New Haven and London: Yale University Press, 1995).

18. Tessa Murdoch, ed., *The Quiet Conquest. The Huguenots, 1685–1985*, (London: Museum of London, 1985), 183.

19. S. Hare, ed., *Paul de Lamérie: At the Sign of the Golden Ball: the Work of England's Master Silversmith*. (London: Goldsmiths' Company, 1990).

20. See Archer, C. "Festoons of flowers . . . For fitting up Print rooms" *Apollo*, vol.130 (1989), 386–391. See also H. Vivarez, *Pro domo mea: Un artiste graveur au XVIIIè siècle, François Vivarès*, (Lille: 1904).

21. Tessa Murdoch, ed., *The Quiet Conquest*, 183. Jean-Baptiste Claude Chatelain was born in London of Huguenot parents. An outstanding landscape engraver, he produced, in 1736, *View at Richmond Palace*, a landscape with a sportsman, and *View of the Thames below Westminster Bridge*.

22. L. Chatelet-Langer, "Salomon De Caus: Contestation d'un Mythe." *Bulletin de la Société Historique des Artistes Français*, 1988, 25–32.

23. Roy Strong, *The Renaissance Garden in England*. (London: Thames and Hudson, 1979).

24. A. Lane, "Daniel Marot: Designer of Delft Vases and of Gardens at Hampton Court." *The Connoisseur*, vol.123, (1949), 19–24.

25. See also Murdoch, *Quiet Conquest*, 186.

Conclusion

This book has detailed the astonishingly large contribution of Huguenots to agriculture, to manufacture and management, to ministry and medicine, to art and invention, and to English-speaking life and culture. It has paid tribute to their descendants, such as Daniel Defoe, author of the novels *Robinson Crusoe* and *Moll Flanders,* as well as the actor David Garrick who played seventeen different roles in Shakespearean plays.[1]

Indeed, the refugees from France frequently had another difficult and paradoxical task to address. For the sake of their integrity, which was the reason why they fled France, they had to be pliant and prepared to adapt their vocations into marketable skills and their way of worshiping in a manner that suited the places where they chose to live.

Except for their political and military influence, the Huguenots exerted far less influence in North America. First, the number of refugees was only approximately between two thousand and ten thousand. Then, their churches often had brief ministries. Consequently, they were strongly laicized, and did not join to form Synods to guide the entire Huguenot congregation in doctrine and worship. In fact, they were almost in a similar position to the Churches of the Désert in eighteenth century France before they were organized by Antoine Court. Furthermore, several ministers became Anglican as did Elie Neau. In addition, the exogamy of Huguenot marriages increased rapidly; for example, between 1720 and 1749, especially when they were performed by Congregational, Presbyterian, and Anglican ministers in New England.[2]

Jon Butler accounts for the vanishing of the French Churches in New York as follows, illustrating three different modes of disappearance—"The failure of dissidents to stand up against Anglican conformity, as at New Rochelle; the failure to preserve any significant French influence in Anglican worship, not even the French language; and the collapse of the independent French congregations in Staten Island and New York City, followed by the dispersal of their members to a broad range of denominations."[3]

After this massive exodus, and because the greater number of those who remained at home went underground or simply abjured their faith, who would have dared to predict a future for Protestantism in France? There were reasons for the perpetration of the Huguenot religion in France. One was that the Camisards believed in answering the sword with the sword and the dragoons with warfare. They managed to defeat the king under Jean Cavalier's leadership. The other involved the sword of the Spirit (Ephesians, 6:17)—that is the word of God—, which sustained people such as Brousson, Corteiz and the Durand family, who supported the great restorer of the Protestant Church, Antoine Court.

Claude Brousson, a lawyer who had organized secret assemblies in the south of France, from 1683 until he was martyred in 1798 at Montpellier, describes eloquently the dangers of these nightly expeditions. He wrote:

> Ordinarily, I camped in the woods, on the mountains, in caves and holes of the earth; often I slept on straw, on a dunghill, on bundles of firewood and amid thorny thickets, on rocks and on the naked earth. During the summer, I was burnt by the blazing sun, and in winter I suffered extreme cold on the mountains covered with snow and ice, not daring to make a fire during the day, afraid that the smoke might discover me; and not daring to leave my hiding place for fear I might be visible to my enemies and false friends. Also sometimes I was exposed to hunger and thirst, and often to overwhelming and deadly exhaustion."[4]

Such witnesses to their faith were the Durand family. The father, Etienne, spent thirteen years in prison, his daughter Marie, was incarcerated for thirty-eight years in the Tour de Constance, and his son Pierre, after many years as a tireless preacher at secret assemblies, was martyred for his beliefs. The quality of their mettle and of their faith is indicated in Pierre's affirmation: "Si mon Sauveur veut m'appeler à signer de mon sang Son Saint Evangile, Sa volonté soit faite." His sister affirmed: "Quand tu me tueras, Seigneur, j'espérerai toujours en toi."[5] Out of such sacrificial spirit, the French Protestant Church could be reborn.

It was revived thanks to Antoine Court to whom the survival of Protestantism in France owes more than to anyone else. Under God, he created a disciplined and dedicated community of Christians, who might otherwise have fallen prey to the idiosyncrasies of wild prophets in the nocturnal gatherings in the Désert of the Cévennes. He preached the necessity of establishing elders in the churches, whose main functions would be to see to the direction of gatherings and the maintenance of pastors, to look after the collection of alms for the poor, to be aware of any scandal and to advise the preachers on all needs of the congregation. In 1730, he escaped to Lausanne, where he created the theological college that he directed for the last thirty years of his life. He occasionally returned to France, despite the risks and the high price promised for his capture, to continue his ministry in the land of the oppressed.[6]

Such missionaries of unyielding faith had no other perspective than the brutal wheel, the gallows or the galleys. Yet, it was such a mixture of courage, vision, and faith that rejuvenated French Huguenots abroad and repristinated French Protestantism in France.

Notes

1. He was buried in Westminster Abbey, appropriately at the foot of Shakespeare's statue.
2. For these years, only three marriages were of French grooms to French brides, while French grooms married ninety English wives and seventy-two English grooms married French brides. See *Reports of the Record Commissioners of the City of Boston*, vol.28. See also Jon Butler, *The Huguenots in America*, (Cambridge, Mass.: Harvard University Press, 1983).
3. Butler, *Huguenots in America*, 189.
4. "The life and ministry of Claude Brousson." *B.H.S.P.F.* vol. 27.
5. Etienne Gammonet, *Etienne Durand et les Siens. (1657–1749)*, (Toulouse: Presses du Languedoc, 1994). Pierre affirmed: "If my Savior chooses to call me to sign his Holy Gospel with my blood, His Will be done." His sister also said "Should you kill me, Lord, I will still put my hope in Thee."
6. Summarized from *Mémoires pour servir à l'histoire et à la vie D'Antoine Court*, 68 ff.

Bibliography

Agnew, David C. A. *Protestant exiles from France.* 3rd ed. Edinburgh: Paterson, 1886.

Arber, Edward. *The Torments of Protestant Slaves in the French King's Galleys and in the Dungeons of Marseilles, 1686–1707 A.D.* London: Privately Printed, 1907.

Aubéry, Jacques. *Histoire de l'Exécution de Cabrières et de Mérindol et d'autres lieux de Provence.* Mérindol, France: Association d'études vaudoises et historiques du Lubéron; Aix-en-Provence: Diffusion, EDISUD,1982.

Auerbach, E. *Tudor Artists.* London: Athlone Press,1954.

Aveling, *The Chamberlens and the Midwifery Forceps,* London: J. & A. Churchill, 1982.

Baird, Charles W. *History of the Huguenot Emigration to America.* New York: Dodd, Mead and Co, 1885.

Baird, Henry M. *History of the rise of the Huguenots of France.* 2 vols. New York: C. Scribners and Sons, 1879. *The Huguenots and the Revocation of the Edict of Nantes.* 2 vols. New York: C. Scribners and Sons, 1895.

Bancroft, George. *History of the United States.* Boston: Little, 1839.

Basnage, Jacques. *Histoire de la religion des églises réformées.* Rotterdam: A. Acher, 1690.

Bastide, Samuel. *Les prisonnières de la Tour de Constance.* Lausanne: Augur, 1957.

Bédard, Marc-André. "La Présence Protestante en Nouvelle France" *Canada's Huguenot Heritage.* Toronto: La Société Historique de Québec, 1978.

Benoit, Daniel. *Du caractère huguenot et des transformations de la piété protestante.* Paris: Fischbacher, 1892.

Benoit, Elie. *History of the Edict of Nantes.* Trans. into English. London: Dunton, 1694.

Bèze, Théodore de, reputed author of *Histoire ecclésiastique des Eglises réformées du royaume de France.* Genève: Droz, 1883. *Psautier de Genève. Les psaumes en vers français: avec leurs mélodies.* Genève: Marot, 1562.

Bien, David. *The Calas Affair: Persecution, Toleration, and Heresy in Eighteenth Century Toulouse.* Princeton, New Jersey: Princeton University Press, 1960.

Bindmau, D. and M. Baker. *Roubiliac and the Eighteenth century Monument: Sculpture as Theatre.* New Haven and London: Yale University Press, 1995.

Bolton, Charles. *Southern Anglicanism. The Church of England in Colonial South Carolina.* Westport, Conn.: Greenwood Press, 1982.

Bost, Charles. *Poésies populaires huguenotes de Vivarais du XVIè. Siècle à la fin de la révolte Camisarde.* Alençon: Corbières et Jugain, 1941.

Bourguet, Pierre. *Huguenots:le Soubriquet mystérieux.* Paris: Collection "Les Bergers et l'Image", 1959.

Boyer, Abel. *A correspondance of Abel Boyer, Huguenot refugee, 1667-1729.* Edited by Rex A. Barrell. Lewiston, New York: E. Mellen Press, 1992.

Brock, Robert A. *Documents, chiefly unpublished, relating to the Huguenot emigration to Virginia and to the settlement at Manakin-Town.* Richmond, Va: Virginia State Library and Archives, 1886.

Browning W. S. *A History of the Huguenots.* Philadelphia: Lee and Blanchard, 1845.

Brousson, Claude. *Etats des Réformés en France.* La Haye?: 1685.

Bulletin de l'histoire de la société du Protestantisme français. Paris: Société du Protestantisme, 1852–.

Bulletin of the Huguenot Society of London.

Butler, Jon. *The Huguenots in America.* Cambridge, Mass.: Harvard University Press, 1983.

Cabanel, Patrick, ed. *Mémoires pour servir à l'histoire et à la vie d'Antoine Court (de 1695 à 1729).* Paris: Editions de Paris, 1995.

Caillot, Antoine. *Morceaux d'éloquence extraits des sermons des orateurs français les plus célèbres au XVIIè siècle précédés à une courte notice sur la vie de chacun d'eux.* Paris: Bruno l'Abbé, 1810.

Charnisay, Madame la baronne de. *Un Gentilhomme Huguenot au temps des Camisards. Le Baron d'Aigaliers.* Mas Soubeyran: Musée du Désert, 1935.

Chenu, Guillaume. *Guillaume Chenu de Chalezac, the "french Boy".* Edited by Randolf Vigne. Capetown: Van Riebeeck Society, 1993.

Chinard, Charles G. *Les Réfugiés huguenots en Amérique.* Paris: "Les Belles Lettres", 1925.

Claude, Jean. *Les plaintes des Protestants cruellement opprimez dans le royaume de France.* Cologne: Pierre Marteau, 1686.

———. *Recueil de Sermons.* Genève: Samuel de Tourne, 1690 and Genève: Collin, 1692.

Colvin, Howard. *A Biographical Dictionary of British Architects. 1600–1800.* 3d ed. Yale: Yale University Press, 1995.

Combe, Ernest. *Les Réfugiés de la Révocation en Suisse.* Lausanne: Georges Bridel, 1885.

Conlon, Pierre. *Jean-François Bion et sa relation des tourments qu'on fait souffrir aux Protestants qui sont sur les galères de France.* Genève: Droz, 1966.

Cooper, W. D. *Lists of Foreign Protestants and Aliens Residents in England, 1618–1685.* London: Westminster Press, 1862.

Coquerel, Athanase J. *Les forçats pour la foi: étude historique, 1684–1787.* Paris: M. Lévy, 1880.

Cotteret, Bernard. *The Huguenots in England: Emigration and Settlement c. 1550–1700*. Cambridge: Cambridge U. P., 1991.

Court, Antoine. *A faithful Account of the Cruelties done to the Protestants*. London: Nutt, 1700.

Davies, Horton. *Worship and Theology in England*. 5 vols. Vols. 2&3, Princeton and Oxford University Presses, 1961–62.

Dearnley, Christopher. *English Church Music, 1650–1750*. London: Barrie and Jenkins, 1970.

Debard, Jean-Marc. *Les Monnaies de la Principauté de Montbéliard du XVIè au XVIIIè Siècle*. Paris: Belles Lettres, 1980.

De Janzé, C. A. *Les Huguenots: Cent Ans de Persécution*. Paris: Grassart, 1886.

Delmas, Louis. *The Huguenots of La Rochelle*. New York: Anson D. F. Randolph and Co., c. 1880.

Didot, *Nouvelle biographie générale*. Paris: Firmin-Didot, 1855.

Dodge, G. H. *The political theory of the Huguenots of the Dispersion with special reference to the thought of Pierre Jurieu*. New York: Columbia U. P., 1947.

Douglas, Donald. *The Huguenot; The Story of the Huguenot Emigrations Particularly to New England*. New York: Dutton, 1954.

Duclos, R. P. *Histoire du protestantisme français au Canada et aux Etats-Unis*. Lausanne: G. Bridel & Co., 1913.

Dupont, Henry. *The story of the Huguenots*. Cambridge, U.S.: Riverside Press, 1982.

Durand. *A Huguenot exile in Virginia Or Voyages of a Frenchman exiled for His Religion With a Description of Virginia & Maryland*. 1687; repr. New York: The Press of the Pioneers, 1934.

Esdaile, Kathleen. *The life and works of Louis-François Roubilliac*. London: Batsford, 1928.

Finney, Paul Corbie, ed. *Seeing beyond the Word*. (see Mentzer Jr., Raymond: The Reformed Churches of France and the Visual Arts) Grand Rapids, Mi.: Eerdmans, 1999.

Fleming, John A. *Huguenot influence in Scotland.* Glasgow: W. Maclellan, 1953.

Flournoy, Jacques. *Journal, 1675–1692.* Genève: Droz, 1994.

Fontaine, Rev. James (compiled by Ann Maury). *Memoirs of a Huguenot family compiled from the original biography and other family Mss.* New York: G. P. Putnam, 1853. Also Bungay: Morrow, 1986.

Foote, W. H. *The Huguenots or Reformed French Church* Richmond, Va.: Presbyterian Committee of Publication, 1870.

Gaillard, Thomas, T. *A Contribution to the History of the Huguenots of South Carolina.* New York: Knickerbocker Press, 1887; reprint: 1972.

Gammonet, Etienne. *Etienne Durand et les siens (1657–1749).* Toulouse: Presses du Languedoc, c.1994.

Gannon, Peter S. ed. *Huguenot refugees in the settling of Colonial America.* New York: The Huguenot Society of America, 1985.

Gilman, C. M. B. *The Huguenot Migration in Europe and in America.* Redbank, N. J.: Arlington Laboratory for Clinical and Historical Research, c.1962.

Goodfriend, Joyce D. *"Too great a mixture of Nations", The Development of New York City Society in the 17th century.* Ph.D. dissertation at Los Angeles: 1975.

Grant, A. J. *The Huguenots.* London: T. Butterworth, 1934.

Gray, Janet G. *The French Huguenots. Anatomy of Courage* Grand Rapids, Mi.: Baker Bookhouse, 1988.

Grey, Irvine R. *Huguenot Manuscripts.* London: Huguenot Society of London, 1983.

Gunnis, Rupert. *Dictionary of British Sculptors. 1660–1851.* London: Odhams Press, 1953.

Gwynn, Robin. *Huguenot Heritage. The History and the Contributions of the Huguenots in Britain.* London: Routledge and Keagan Paul, 1985.

Haag, Eugène and Emile. *La France protestante*. 5 Vols. Paris: Fischbacher, 1877–86.

Hare, S., ed., *Paul de Lamérie: At the Sign of the Golden Ball: the Work of England's Master Silversmith*. London: Goldsmiths' Company, 1990.

Heath, Richard. *The Reformation in France from the dawn of Reform to the Revocation of the Edict of Nantes* London: Religious Tract Society, 1886.

Hilliard, N. *A Treatise concerning the Arte of Limning* Reprint: Ashington Northumberland: Mid-Northumberland Arts Group, 1981.

Hind, C. *The Rococo in England*. London: Victoria and Albert Museum, 1986.

Hirsch, A. H. *The Huguenots of Colonial South Carolina* Durham, N. C.: Duke University Press, 1928.

———. *Histoire de la persécution faite à l'Eglise de Rouen sur la fin du dernier siècle*. Rotterdam: 1704. Reprinted Rouen: L. Deshays, 1874.

Howells, R. J. *Pierre Jurieu Antinomian Radical*. Durham: University of Durham, 1983.

———. *Les Huguenots. Exposition nationale*. Paris: Archives Nationales, Documentation française, 1985–86.

———. *The Hymn: A Journal of Congregational Song*. 48 vols.

Isambert, François-A. *Recueil général des anciennes lois françaises*. 29 Vols. Paris: Belin-le-Prieur, 1821–33.

Jacquelot de Chantemerle de Vilette, Patrice. *Les Jacquelot Protestants du XVIè au XVIIIè siècle en Champagne et dans les Pays Etrangers*. Paris: Chez l'auteur, 1994.

Jones E. A. *The old silver Sacramental Vessels of foreign Protestant Churches in London*. London: J. M. Dent, 1908.

Jurieu, Pierre. *La politique du clergé de France ou Entretiens curieux de deux catholiques romains . . . sur les moyens dont on se sert aujourd'huy pour destruire la religion protestante dans ce royaume*. Cologne?: 1681.

Kershen, Anne J., ed. *London the promised land?: the migrant experience in a capital city.* Aldershot, Hants & Brookfield, Vermont: Avebury, 1997.

Knox, S. J. *Ireland's debt to the Huguenots.* Dublin: APCK, 1959.

Latreille, A. *Histoire de Lyon et du Lyonnais.* Genève: Famot, 1976.

Lavender, Abraham D. *French Huguenots. From Mediterranean Catholics to White Anglo-Saxon Protestants.* New York: P. Lang, 1990.

Lecky, W. E. *History of Ireland.* London: Longmans Green, 1913.

Lee, Grace Lawless. *The Huguenot Settlements in Ireland* London: Longmans, 1936.

Léonard, Emile G. *Le Protestant Français.* Paris: P.U.F., 1955.

Ligou, Daniel. *Le Protestantisme en France de 1590 à 1715.* Paris: Société d'Edition d'Enseignement Supérieur, 1968.

Liturgy, or Forms of divine service translated from the liturgy of the church of Neufchatel and Vallagin the whole adapted to publick worship in the United States of America. 3d ed. New York: A.D. Randolph, 1853.

The Liturgy or Forms of Divine service of The French Protestant Church of Charleston, S.C. Charleston, S. C.: Walker and James, 1953.

Lorimer, J. G. *An Historical Sketch of the Protestant Church of France.* Philadelphia: Presbyterian Board of Publication, 1842.

Louis XIV. Ed. Lognon, ed. *Mémoires.* Paris: Tallandier, 1978.

Macpherson, David. *Annals of Commerce.* London: Nichols and Son, 1805.

Mandrou, R & Alii. *Histoire des Protestants de France.* Toulouse: Privat, 1977.

Marot, Clément. *Fifty Psalms.* Paris: Bogard, 1545.

Marteilhe, J. *Mémoires d'un Protestant condemné aux galères de France pour cause de Religion écrits par lui-même* Rotterdam: 1755 and London: Griffiths and Dilly, 1758.

Mémoires inédits d'Abraham Mazel et d'Elie Marin sur la Guerre des Cévennes. Paris: Fischbacher, 1931.

Mention, Léon. *Documents relatifs aux rapports du clergé avec la royauté*. Genève: Stakine-Megeriotis, 1976.

Michaud, Jean. *Histoire: 1492-1789. La Renaissance et les Temps Modernes*. Paris: Hachette, 1970.

Michelet, Jules. *Louis XIV et la Révocation de l'Edit de Nantes*. Paris: Flammarion, 1898-99.

Migault, Jean. *Journal de Jean Migault ou malheurs d'une famille protestante du Poitou (1682-1689*. Paris: Editions de Paris, 1995.

———. *Minutes of the Consistory of the French Church of London, Threadneedle St., 1679-1692*. London: Huguenot Society, 1994.

Miquel, Pierre. *Histoire de la France*. Paris: Fayard, 1976.

Moens, W. J. C. *The Walloons and their church at Norwich, 1565-1832*. Lymington: Huguenot, Society of London, 1888.

Mornay, Arbaleste de. *A Huguenot Family in the XVIth century: The memoirs of Philippe de Mornay*. London: Routledge, 1926.

Mousnier, Roland. *Histoire générale des civilizations*, Paris: P.U.F., 1967.

Mours, S. *Les Eglises Réformées en France*. Paris and Strasbourg: Librairie Protestante, 1958.

Murdoch, Tessa. *The Quiet Conquest. The Huguenots, 1685-1985*. London: Museum of London, 1985.

Orcibal, Jean. *Etat présent des recherches sur la répartition géographique des "nouveaux catholiques" à la fin du XVIIè siècle*. Paris: Vrin, 1948.

Patouillet, Etienne. *Oraison funèbre de Marie-Thérèse d'Autriche*. Besançon: Rigoine, 1683.

Perry, Elizabeth I. *From Theology to History: French Religious Controversy and the Revocation of the Edict of Nantes*. La Hague: M. Nijhof 1973.

Poole, R. L. *A History of the Huguenots of the dispersion to the Recall of the Edict of Nantes*. London: Macmillan, 1880.

Pidoux, Pierre. Loys Bourgeois' Abteil am Hugenotten-Psalter. *Jahrbuch für Liturgik und Hymnologie*, 15. Kassel: J. Standa, 1970.

Powell, John Stocks. *Huguenots Planters. Port Arlington*: York: French Church Press, 1994..

Proceedings of the Huguenot Society of London

Proceedings of the Huguenot Society of America. New York: The Society . . . , 1896–.

Raoul, Stéphane. *L'Epopée huguenote*. Paris: Colombe, 1945.

Reaman, G. Elmore. *The Trail of the Huguenots in Europe, in the United States, South Africa and Canada*. London and Baltimore: Genealogical Publications, 1963.

Reymond, Bernard. *L'architecture religieuse des protestants*. Geneva: Labor et Fides, 1996.

Roche, Owen I. A. *The days of the upright; the story of the Huguenots*. New York: C.H. Potter, 1965.

Rothrock, George A. *The Huguenots: A Biography of a Minority*. Chicago: Nelson Hall, 1979.

Rousset, Camille F. M. *Histoire de Louvois de son administration politique et militaire*. 4 vols. Paris: Didier, 1862–64.

Rulhière, Claude de. *Eclaircissements historiques sur les causes de la Révocation de l'Edit de Nantes et sur l'état des Protestants en France*. Genève: F. Dufart, 1788.

Saillens, Ruben. *The Soul of France*. London: Morgan and Scott, 1916.

Schickler, F.D.G. de. *Les Eglises de Refuge en Angleterre*. Paris: Fischbacher, 1892.

Scouloudi, Irène. *Huguenots in Britain and their French background*. London: Basingstoke: Macmillan, 1987.

Scoville, Warren C. *The persecution of Huguenots and French economic development, 1680–1720*. Berkeley: University of California, 1960.

Simms, W. G. *Huguenots in Florida: a series of sketches . . . 1562–1570*. 3d ed. New York: Baker and Scribner, 1854.

Smedley, Edward. *History of the Reformed Religion in France* New York: Harper Bros., 1834.

Smiles, Samuel. *The Huguenots: their settlements, churches and industries in England and Ireland*. London, 1880; New York: Harper Bros., 1867.

Souchal, F. *French Sculptors of the Age of Louis XIV*. 4 vols. Paris and Oxford: Cassirer, 1977.

Strong, Roy. *The Renaissance Garden in England*. London: Thames and Hudson, 1979.

Sutherland, N. M. *The Huguenot struggle for recognition*. New Haven: Yale University Press, 1980.

Tournier, G. *Les Galères de France et les galériens Protestants des XVIIè et XVIIIè siècles*. Le Mas Soubeyran: Musée du Désert: 1943.

Transactions of the Huguenot Society of South Carolina. Charleston: Walker, Evans & Cogswell.

Verge-Franceschi, Michel. *Abraham Du Quesne, Huguenot et Marin du Roi-Soleil*. Paris: France-Empire, 1992.

Waterhouse, Ellis. *Painting in Britain*. London: Penguin Book, 1953.

Weiss, Charles. *A History of the French Protestant Refugees from the Revocation of the Edict of Nantes to Our Own Days*. New York: Stringer and Townsend, 1854.

Wright, Christopher. *The French Painters of the Seventeenth Century*. New York: Graphic Society/Little Brown, 1985.

Zoff, Otto. *The Huguenots: fighters for God and Human Freedom*. New York: L. B. Fischer, 1942.

Index

Abbadie, 50, 67, 78–80
Abbé de Cheyla, 22
Abbeville, 50
Abjuration, abnegation, 8,11–12, 60–61, 75–76, 114
Académie Royale de Peinture (1648–), 111
Agnew, 96
Alamanza, 87
Alençon, 60
Algiers, 46
Allix, Pierre, 50, 67, 79
Alsace, 9
Alvert, Pierre, 105
America, 39, 45, 85, 95, 98, 104, 106
Amiens, 82
Amsterdam, 49, 101
Amyand, Claudius, 84
Amyrault, Moyse, 68
Andouet, James, 101
Anglivielle, Marguerite, 28
Angoumois, province of, 99
Anjou, 46
Anne, queen of England, 103
Antilles, 44, 90, 106–07
Apparel, 95–96, 99–101
Archambo, Peter, 103
Architects, ch. 7
Armagh, 80
Arminianism, 68
Artists, ch. 7
Attractions of foreign lands, 39–45, 50–51

Audubert, Anne, 33
Augustine, St., 66
Auvergne, province of, 99

Ballou, 90
Bangor, 82
Banking, 105–06
Baptism, 8–9, 63, 64
Basnage, 67, 68, 80
Baudin, admiral, 30
Baudoin, Christopher, 102
Baudoin, René, 106
Bauhin, Jean, 82
Baux, G., 50
Bawdoin, 85
Béarn, 4, 7
Beauregard, P. L., 25
Beauveau, count, 86
Benoit, Daniel, 62
Benoit, Elie, 45, 80
Benzeville, Esther, 48
Béraud, Marie, 28
Berlin, 50, 78
Bernard, Jacques-Samuel, 112
Berne, canton, 40 (see also Switzerland)
Bernon, Gabriel, 106–07
Berry, 40
Bertheau, 66
Besançon, 8
Bèza, Théodore de, 63, 64
Bèzenet, Anthony, 79
Bible, x, 62
Bion, Jean, 31

Bombelle, 29
Bordeaux, 29, 41
    Academy of, 97
Bosanquet, David, 105, 106
Bossuet, Archbishop, 6, 67, 79, 86
Boston, 44, 60, 67, 80, 105, 106
Boudinot, 90
Bouhéreau, Elie 21, 81, 85
Bouillon, Duke of, 68
Bourgeois, 64
Bourgeois, Louis, 111
Boussière, Paul, 84
Bowdoin, 85
Boyceau, Jacques, 111
Boyer, Abel, 85
Brandenburg, 11, 51, 86, 98
Brest, 29, 100
Brighton, 82
Britain and England, ix, 62, 82, 83f., 95-98, 100-04, 111
Britanny, 28, 41, 99-100
Brosse, Abraham, 112
Brousson, 12, 26 (see also Camisards)
Buissière, Paul, 84

Caillemotte, 86, 87
Caisse des conversions, 20-21
Calais, 50
Calas, Jean, 13, 21
Calvin, 22, 63, 64, 104
Calvinism, x, 22, 60, 62-69, 104
Camabon, 87
Cambridge University, 72, 79, 81
Camisards, 12f., 26, 80
Canada, 107
Canterbury, 42, 81
Cappel, James, 80
Carignan, 86
Caroline, queen of England, 84
Cartier, Jean, 103
Cateau-Cambrésis, treaty of, 2
Catholic(s), *passim*
    holidays, 61
Caudebec, 95
Cavalier, Jean, 12
Cévennes, 12, 40-41, 83

Chaigneau, Andrew, 102
Chamberlain, Guillaume & Pierre (s), 82-83, 98
Champagne, province of, 40, 99
Champion, Néhémiah, 96
Channel Isles, 40, 46, 100
Chardin, Jean, 84
Charenton, 22, 65-66, 78, 80
Charles I, king of England, 103
Charles II, king of England, 83, 87, 111
Charleston, 44, 45, 98, 105
Charlotte-Amélie, queen of Denmark, 80
Chassereau, Francis, 102
Chatellerault, 105
Chatillon-sur-Loing, academy of, 6, 86
Chelsea, 87, 103
Chénevix, Paul Daniel, 103
Chester, 82
Children, x, 6, 10, 20,
Church architecture, 64-66
Church vessels, 66
Claude, Jean, 22, 66-69, 81
Cloth and apparel industry, 95-96, 99-101
Cloudesley, Paul, 102
Colbert, 5, 8, 9, 98
Coligny, 6
Colladon, Jean & Théodore, 83
Collin, Dr., 2
Colomies, Paul, 85
Comtesse, 90
Condé, prince of, 4, 87
Consistory, 8, 64
Constance, Tower of, 27-28, 57
Conversion, 6
Copenhagen, 88
Copernicus, 97
Coqueux, Antoine, 83
Cork, 87
Cosme, 8
Court, Antoine, 12-13, 28, 58, 68
Courtauld (family), 102
Cousin, Jean, 111
Crespin, Paul, 103

Crommelin (family), 42, 101
Cuissi, 87
Cuny, Louis, 103

D'Aigaliers, baron, 27
    Madame, 27
Daillé, 67, 80f.
Danthon, 102
D'Arsellières, Marcus, 87
D'Aubigné, 4
D'Aubigné, Merle, 81
Daubuz, Charles, 79
Dauphiné, province of, 40–41, 68
De Baufré (family), 103
De Baulieu, Luke, 79
De Brosse, Salomon, 111
De Charmes, Simon, 103
De Cloux, Peter, 102
De Cosnac, Daniel, 22
De Fay, Jacques, 105
De Gassion, count, 86
De la Cave, count, 86
De la Chaumette, Isaac, 96
De la Fausille, René, 87
De La Force, duke, 86
De La Noix, 90
De la Rochefoucauld, 48
De la Trimeville, duke, 86
De Lalo, Samson, 87
De Lamérie, Paul, 103
De Lancey (family) 106
De Landreville, Noël, 99
De l'Angle, 79
De Laune, Gidéon, 82
De l'Etang, 87
De Limarest, Thomas, 102
De Maizaux, Peter, 85
De Manoir, R. L., 96
De Maranic, comte, 46
De Marillac, intendant, 7, 32
De Marolles, Louis, 30
De Mayerne, Sir Theodore Turquet, 83
De Moivre, Abraham, 85
De Mouginot, François, 84
De Neufville, baron, 23
De Robillard, 49

De Rohan, duke, 86
De Rouffignac, 58
De Roye, count, 86
De Ruvigny, Henri de Massue, 49, 87
De Sévigné, Madame, 9, 79
De Varennes, marquis, 86
De Vaux, Gérard, 90, 104
Decatur, 88
Defoe, 71, 125
Dehaufré, Jacob & Peter, 103
Delaware, 44
Delorme, 65
Denew, James, 106
Denmark, 80, 88
Deportation, 10, 87–88
Derby, 103
Désaguliers, Jean Théophilus, 84, 96
Désert, Church of the, 10, 106
Dewey, 88
Deyoin, 68
Dezouch, 101
Dié, 24, 67, 68
Digue, James, 101
Disguises and modes of escaping, 46–50
D'Olier, Isaac & Jeremiah, 101
Dollond, John, 95
Dortrecht, Synod of, 68
Dover, 40
Dragonnades and dragoons, 22–26
Drelincourt, Charles, 67, 79, 84
Drelincourt, dean, 80, 84
Droilhet (family), 106
Du Bosc, Pierre, 68
Du Bourg, Ann, 2
Du Cerceaux, Jacques, 112
Du Parc, Boyer, 4
Du Perrier, Antoine, 87
Du Plessis Gauret, 86
Du Quesne, admiral, 7, 10, 20, 26, 86, 88
Du Vivier, Marie-Ann, 60
Dubison, Peter, 96
Dublin, 62, 78, 80–85 *passim*
Dubourdieu, Izaac & Jean Armand, 79
Dumouslin, Louis, 67, 85

Dunkirk, 28
Duplaix, Claude, 102
Durand, David, 79, 84
Durand, Marie, 28
Durel, 77
Dusson, 63
Dutch, 100-101
Duval, Philip, 79

Ecrivain, Jean, 33
Edicts
    of Alès (1629), 4
    for the kidnapping of Children (1681), 50
    of Nantes (1598) ix, x, 3-4, 6
    Revocation of (1685), x, 1, 2, 21-22, 26, 67, 88
    of Toleration (1787), x, 13-14
Edinburgh, 82, 100
Edward VI, king of England, 41
Elfin, 82
Elizabeth, queen of England, 41, 62
Elle the Elder, Louis Ferdinand, 112
Emigration, 9-10, ch. 2, 19f.
Engineering, 96-98
England, (see Britain and London)
    Bank of, 104, 106
Erlanger, 57
Esselbroun, Jean, 105
Evelyn, the diarist, 98
Exeter, 49

Fabre, Jean, 31
Faith, x, 63, 69, 71, 77
Falmouth, 49
Faneuil brothers, 104, 106
Farges, Pierre, 22
Faucette, Rachael, 90
Flanders, 88
Fonant & Roberts, informers, 11
Fonnereaus, 103
Fontaine, James, 67, 84
Foubert, H., 87
Foucault, 7
France, *passim*
Frankfurt, 63
Fredrick, William, Elector of Prussia, 43, 78

Fronde, 4
Fulda river, 97

Gabaret, Jean, 88
Gagnier, Jean, 80, 85
Gallaudet, Thomas H, 85
Galleys, x, 10, 26-32, 76
    march to, 27-29
Gambier, admiral, 88
Gardening, 101
Garnier, Daniel, 103
Garrick, 71
Gauge, 97
Gaussainte, Anne, 28
Geneva, 1, 40, 63, 68-69, 98
George II, king of England, 97
Georgetown, 45
Germany, (see also Hesse & Prussia), 86
Gervase, Louis, the Younger, 105
Gex, 7, 98
Gibraltar, 87
Giles, James, 104
Gloucester, cathedral, 79, 80
Gorge, Jacques, 99
Goujon, Jean, 111
Goulon, 87
Grabu, Louis, 111
Grenoble, 8
Gribelin, Simon, 103
Grignion, Thomas, 103
Grostête de la Mothe, Claude, 79
Gruche, Pierre, 98
Guébriant, marshal, 86
Guérard, Jacob, 105
Guérard, Peter Jacob, 98
Guernsey Island, 40, 97, 105
Guichard, Mlle, 48
Guizot, 33
Guyenne, 40
Guyon, Daniel, 101
Gwynn, Robin, 39, 70, 107

Hackensack, 80
Hamilton, Alexander, 89
Harrache, Pierre the Elder & Pierre the Younger, 103
Harrache, Thomas, 103

Index

Henrietta-Maria, queen of England, 83, 98
Henry III, king of France, 2
Henry IV (from Navarre), king of France, 2, 3, 20, 68, 111
Hesse, 86
Holland, (see also Dutch) ix, 11, 40, 65-67, 80, 86, 97, 100-04 *passim*
Hooke, Robert, 97
Houblon, Sir John, 106
Hoxton, 66
Huguenot, *passim*
   academies, 4, 7-8, 20-24, 68-69, 79
   beliefs, 57-58, 70
   character, x, ch. 4 *passim*, 61-63, 69-71, 107, 126
   discipline, 5, 58, 61, 70
   exclusion from charges and offices, 7
   harassment and persecutions, 5, 19-20
   military, 85-88
   ministers, x, ch. 5, 66-67
   numbers who escaped, 39
   politicians, 89-90
   prisons for women, 27

Ile de France, province of, 40
Immigrants' roots, 40-41
Incarceration, 26-28
Indians, 107
Informers, 11
Inventions 95-98, 104, 125
Inventors and Manufacturers, ch. 6
Ireland, ix, 50, 62, 78, 80, 86-87, 95, 100-103
   Bank of, 106
Islington, 97
Italy, 86

James I, king of England, 82, 83
James II, king of England, 41, 49
Jamets, 6
Jansen, Théodore, 106
Jansenists, persecutions of, x, 5, 68
Jay, John, 89

Jersey, 40, 112
Jewel, Bishop, 62
Jonjac, 81
Jortin, John, 79
Jumineau, Daniel, 105
Jurieu, Pierre, 67-68, 79
Justel, Henri, 84

Killaloe, 50, 78

La Chaumette, Isaac, 96
La Fabrèque, 87
La Haye, 49, 67
La Mellonière, 87
La Rochelle, 1, 4, 6, 21, 44, 48, 51, 65, 67, 69, 89, 96, 106
La Touche, D. (family), 83, 89
La Touche, Digges, 106
La Tremblade, 51
Laforey, J. and F., 88
Landerneau, 100
L'Anglais, Philippe, 106
Languedoc, province of, 41
Lanson, 102
Latigue, 101
Latore, 101
Laurens, Henry, 90
Lausanne, 40, 63, 67
Lavalade, Charles, 101
Le Blond, James Christopher, 96, 102
Le Boyne, battle of, 87
Le Camus, Etienne, 22
Le Clerc, Pierre, 101
Le Fanu, W. R., 83
Le Faucheur, Michel, 68
Le Fèbvre, Roland, 112
Le Fèvre, Nicolas, 83
Le Mann, 95
Le Mans, 102
Le Marchand, David, 103
Le Moine, 79
Le Nain, brothers, 112
Le Roux, 101
Le Vasseur, Michel, 85
League to oppose France's religious policies, 11
Lee, G.L., 62

Leeds, 105
Legaré de Longuemare, Solomon & Nicholas, 105
Leiden, 81
Léman, James, 102
Lestourgeon, David, 103
Lethieullier, Samuel, 106
Ligonier, marshal, and family, 71, 87–88
Lille, 102
Lisburn, 101
Lisy, 80
Locke
  philosophy, 13
  visit to France, 19–20
London, 40, 50, 60, 80, 98, 102–06
  British Museum, 84
  House of Commons, 89, 96
  Hoxton Square, 80
  Lambeth Palace, 85
  Pall Mall, 103
  Planetarium, 96
  Royal Bounty, 43
  Royal Exchange, 95
  Royal Society, 84, 96–98,
  Sallow Street, 96
  Savoy Church, 50
  St James Chapel, 76
  St James, Library, 85
  St. Paul's Cathedral, 81, 82
  Strand, the, 104
  Threadneedle Street Church, 79, 105
Lord Proprietors, 105, 106
Lordell, John, 106
Lorraine, duke of, 86
Loubiers, 106
Louis XIII, king of France, 3, 4, 111
Louis XIV, king of France, 4, 5, 86–88, 98–99, 102–7, 111
  efforts to convert Schomberg, 5
  methods for religious unification, 4–7
  struggles with papacy, 5
Louvois, 5, 8, 10
Lunel, 61
Lunel, Pierre, 88

Luther, 22
Lyon, 33, 64, 65, 99

MacPherson, 100
Magdebourg, 88
Magendie, W., 82
Maine, province of, 100
Mallard, Michael, 79
Malplaquet, 87
Manchester, 81
Manufactures 9, ch. 6, 98f., 125
Marguerite, queen of Navarre, 82
Marine, 49
Mariotte, 97
Mariscot, 102
Marlborough, duke of, 88
Marly, 2
Marot, Clément, 63, 64, 111
Marot, Daniel, 104–05
Marriage Service, 64,
Marseilles, 28–29
Martheille, 28–29
Martin, 80
Martineau, Arthur & Gaston, 81, 84
Martineau, James, 81, 84
Martinique, 32
Mary, queen of England, 62
Mascarene, Jean, 59
Mas-d'Azil, 75
Massey, Henry & Jacob, 103
Maty, Matthieu, 84
Mazyk, Izaac (of South Carolina), 45
Mazyk, Stephen (of Ireland), 42
Meaux, 1
Medici, Marie de, regent of France, 4
Mesnard, 67
Métrezat, Jean, 68
Metz, 102
Meynard, John and Philippe, 80
Michelin, Jean, 112
Military, 85–88
Minet, 106
Miniature, 112–14
Minorca, 87
Molinist, 68
Moncal, Mark, 87
Monceux, 102

Monlon, Pierre, 98
Montague, E.W., 62, 95
Montauban, 4, 20, 23, 68-69
Montpellier, 7, 19, 27, 67, 89
Morlaix, 100
Mouret, Mme, 27
Mours, S., 40
Musicians, 111

Naarden, 86
Nantes, 100
    edict of Nantes (1598), see Edict
National Unity, ix-x, 1, 3-6 *passim*, 9, 10
Navy (see also ships) 87-89
Neau, Elie, 30
Neufchatel, 68
New Amsterdam, 44
New Oxford, 107
New Paltz, 44, 67
New Rochelle, 44
New York, 80. 99. 106
    Columbia University, 90
Newman, cardinal, 81
Newton, 97
Nîmes, 6, 8, 10, 62, 68
Niort, 25
Normandy (province of), 40, 99-100
Norwich, 84

Obedience, 1
Obrisset, John, 103
Obstetric forceps, 83
Ogier (family), 102
Onge, Daniel, 102
Orange, 21
Origen, 21
Orléans, 2
Orthez, 67, 68
Oxford, 77, 79, 85, 97
Ozier, 101

Palissy, Bernard, 111
Pallet, John, 101
Papin, Denis, 83-84, 97-98
Paris, 2, 6, 47, 80, 83, 99
Pascall, James, 105

Patouillet, Bishop, 8
Pelissier, Abel, 87
Pelissier, Alexandre, 101
Pelisson-Fontanier, 20
Pelletier (family), 105
Pennète, Raymond, 101
Pennsylvania, (see also Philadelphia), 107
Perronet, Vincent, 79
Persecutions, x, 2, 6, 9, 13, ch. 2
Pershing, general, 88
Petit, Louis, 87
Philadelphia, 90
Physicians and medicine, 21, 82-85
Picardy, province of, 40, 101
Pigganet, Bertrand, 101
Platel, Pierre, 103
Plymouth, 40, 46
Politics and politicians, 1-4, 89-90
Pons, 28, 81
Pontarlington, 101, 103
Poole, R.L., 39
Pope, 1
    struggles with Louis XIV, 3, 5
Portal, Henry, 104
Portalès, Charles, 83
Pousset, Francis, 96
Prayers, x
Predestination, doctrine of, 57
Primerose, surgeon, 83
Printers and bookbinders, 104
Prioleau, Elie, 81
Prioleau, Elizea, 81
Privas, 4
Privat, Edouard, 59
Protestant, *passim*
Protestantism, ix-x, 104, 106
Provence, province of, 41
Providence, Rhode Island, 107
Prussia, ix, 62, 63, 95
Psalmody, 64
Puritans, 62
Pusey, Edward Bouverie, 81
Puylaurens, 67

Québec, 43
Quévilly, 65

Rabelais, 79
Raboteau, J.C., 101
Racine, Benjamin, 101
Ramsey Castle, 23
Raper, Matthew, 103
Reconnaissance, services of, 60
Regis, Balthazar, 79
Revere, Paul, 105
Revocation of the Edict of Nantes
    (see Edicts)
Rhode Island, 4, 21
Richard, Elie, 21
Richelieu, 4, 86
Rieutort, 87
Rivière, Robert, 104
Rivoire, Apollos, 105
Rochette, pastor, 13, 61
Rocroi, battle of, 86
Roget, Peter Mark, 84, 98
Romaine, William, 82
Romilly, Samuel, 66, 75, 89
Rotterdam, 66, 81
Rouen, 65, 79, 102
Roussel, Mary, 48
Roye, count of, 86
Royal Bounty, 43
Royan, 51
Ruvigny, marshal, 20, 45
Rye, 40

Sabatier, 31
Saint Amand, Penrose, 104
Saint Malo, 40
Sainte-Marie, Lewis Anne, 96
Saint-Evremont, 83-85
Saintonge, province of, 41
Saint-Simon, 9
Salem, 51, 106
San Domingo, 32
Saumur, 7, 21, 67-69, 79-80, 104
Saurin, 67, 81
Savery, Thomas, 96, 97
Savoy, duke of, 87
Schley, 88
Schomberg, marshal, 6, 20, 67, 78,
    86, 87
Scotland, 100

Sculptors, 117-120, 122
Sedan 68-69, 79
Seignelet, 5, 8, 9, 88
Seignette, 21
Seignoret, Etienne, 105
Sermons, 1-8, 68f.
Serres, Daniel, 27
Shérard, William, 102
Ships, 10, 29-31, 40, 45-49
    passim, 106-07
Silversmiths and goldsmiths, 102-03,
    105, 119-121 *passim*
Silvestre, Pierre, 84
Six, James, 96
Slavery, 32
Sommiers, 49
Soret, 101
Sortain, Joseph, 82
South Africa, Huguenot settlement in,
    ix, 43
South Carolina, 45, 98, 105
Southampton, 40
Spendau, 86
Sprimont, Nicholas, 103
St Bartholomew Massacre, 83
Staten Island, 80
Sully, 4, 20
Sweden, 11
Switzerland, 39, 40, 63, 68, 98

Tarentum, prince of, 86
Telescope, 95
Terrasson, Jean, 50
Terrot, Charles H., 82
Testelin (brothers), Henri & Louis,
    112
Thackeray, W.M., 92
Tillières, informer, 11
Torbay, 86
Touraine, province of, 41
Touton, Jean, 44
Tractarian movement, 81
Trench, P. le Poer, 82
Trench, R. C., 82
Trimeville, duke of, 86
Trompe-l'oeil, 111
Tuam, 82

Tucker, 70
Turenne, 6, 20, 87

Utrecht, 81
Uzès, 62

Vaillant, François, 104
Valence, 22
Vansommer, Jean, 102
Vauban, 9, 98, 100
Vaut Rollier, Thomas, 104
Vence, D.B.B., 40
Versailles, 88
Vialès, Noah, 101
Victoria, queen of England, 104
Vidouse, James, 102
Vigiem, James River, 62
Vigne, Jaquette, 28
Virgin, cult of the, 1
Virginia, 107
Vivarais, 10
Vivennes, 12
Voltaire, 10

Wake, 79
Waldenses, 1
Walloons, 41, 100
Wandsworth, 95
Wars of Religion, 1,
    Civil wars of religions 2-3, 10
    Sedition, 12
Waterford, 101
Waterford, W., 7
Weiss, Charles, historian, 39
Wheel, torture of the, 34
Wilberforce, 87, 89
Wilhemina, princess of Wales, 103
Willaume, David, 103
William III, (prince of Orange) and
    Mary, king and queen of
    England, 11, 42, 43, 80,
    86, 99, 101
Windsor, 67
Worship and places of worship, 3, 6-
    9 *passim*, 19, 40, 63-65,
    76-78
Wriothesley, Thomas, 87

Studies in Church History

This series in Church History offers a place for diverse scholarship that is sometimes too particularly calibrated for any other publishing category. Rather, the richness of the Church History series is in its scope which variously mixes historical theology and historical hermeneutics, doctrine and practices of piety, religious or spiritual movements, and institutional configurations. Western Europe and the United States continue to provide grounds for exploration and discourse, but this series will also publish books on Christianity in Asia, Africa, and Latin America. Traditional periodization (Early Christian, Medieval, Reformation and Modern eras) grants maximum representation.

The particular focus of the series is the treatment of religious thought as being vital to the historical context and outcome of Christian experience. Fresh interpretations of classic and well-known Christian thinkers (e.g., Augustine, Luther, Calvin, Edwards, etc.) using multicultural perspectives, the critical approaches of feminist and men's studies form the foundation of the series. Meanwhile, new voices from Christian history need illumination and explication by church historians in this series. Authors who are versatile enough to "cross-over" disciplinary boundaries have enormous opportunity in this series to reach an international audience.

For inquiries, please contact the series editor:

Dr. William L. Fox
Department of Philosophy
Montgomery College
20200 Observation Dr.
Germantown, MD 20875

To order other books in this series, please contact our Customer Service Department at:

(800) 770-LANG (within the U.S.)
(212) 647-7706 (outside the U.S.)
(212) 647-7707 FAX

or browse online by series at:

www.peterlang.com

Studies in Church History

General Editor: William L. Fox

This series in Church history offers a place for diverse scholarship that is sometimes too particularly calibrated for any other publishing category. Rather, the richness of the Church history series is in its scope, which variously mixes historical theology and historical hermeneutics, doctrine and practices of piety, religious or spiritual movements, and institutional configurations. Western Europe and the United States continue to provide grounds for exploration and discourse, but this series will also publish books on Christianity in Asia, Africa, and Latin America. Traditional periodization (Early Christian, Medieval, Reformation and Modern eras) grants maximum representation.

The particular focus of the series is the treatment of religious thought as being vital to the historical context and outcome of Christian experience. Fresh interpretations of classic and well-known Christian thinkers (e.g., Augustine, Luther, Calvin, Edwards, etc.) using multicultural perspectives, the critical approaches of feminist and men's studies form the foundation of the series. Meanwhile, new voices from Christian history need illumination and explication by church historians in this series. Authors who are versatile enough to "cross-over" disciplinary boundaries have enormous opportunity in this series to reach an international audience.

For additional information about this series or for the submission of manuscripts, please contact:
>Peter Lang Publishing
>Acquistions Dept.
>516 N. Charles St., 2nd Floor
>Baltimore, MD 21201

To order other books in this series, please contact our Customer Service Department at:
>(800) 770-LANG (within the U.S.)
>(212) 647-7706 (outside the U.S.)
>(212) 647-7707 FAX

or browse online by series at:
>WWW.PETERLANG.COM